A Guide to Parliamentary Procedure for Local Governments in Wisconsin

Larry E. Larmer
Division of Continuing Studies
University of Wisconsin-Madison

KENDALL/HUNT PUBLISHING COMPANY
4050 Westmark Drive Dubuque, Iowa 52002

ISBN 0-7872-5533-5

Printed in the United States of America
10 9 8 7 6 5 4

TABLE OF CONTENTS

ACKNOWLEDGMENTS

If this booklet does not accomplish its aim, the author bears sole responsibility. But if this reference is helpful, it was made so by many who generously provided guidance and feedback during its preparation. Grateful acknowledgment is extended to:

Alan M. Abramson, Former Assistant Chief Clerk, Montana House of Representatives

Professor Michael R. Chial, Department of Professional Development and Applied Studies, University of Wisconsin-Madison

Rollie Cox, Professional Registered Parliamentarian, Past-President, National Association of Parliamentarians

Professor David G. Hinds, Director, Local Government Center, University of Wisconsin-Extension

Patricia L. Malone, Community Natural Resource and Economic Development Agent, Trempeleau County, University of Wisconsin-Extension

Professor David L. Vancil, Department of Speech Communication, Colorado State University, Fort Collins, Colorado and Past President, Commission on American Parliamentary Practice

Professor Fred A. Wileman, Department of Professional Development and Applied Studies, University of Wisconsin-Madison

Peter Williams, Former Board President, Madison (Wisconsin) Metropolitan School District

Jane A. Wilms, Clerk, Village of Germantown, Wisconsin

But those most responsible for any usefulness this booklet may have are the many elected and employed members of units of local governments in Wisconsin who are attentive to parliamentary procedure as an instrument of democracy. The author is privileged to have been involved with them in a challenging and productive dialogue over the years.

INTRODUCTION

This booklet is a guide to parliamentary procedure. It is designed especially for officials of local governments in Wisconsin who are often faced with questions of procedure that are not easily answered by manuals such as *Robert's Rules of Order Newly Revised.*

Officials of local governments need to follow good, clear rules of procedure. Such rules promote fairness, equality, and order so that members of local government units can deliberate on equal footing and so that their constituents will be fairly represented.

But local government officials have professional lives of their own and their service to their community is extended on a low paying or even volunteer basis. To expect them to have acquired a thorough knowledge of parliamentary procedure is unrealistic. They need — and deserve — an easy-to-use reference guide.

Accordingly, this booklet aspires to provide a convenient first step in resolving those questions of procedure that are not grounded in statute or in the group's own rules. It is based on the Robert's tradition and echoes many of the precepts contained in *Robert's Rules of Order Newly Revised.* But this guide is narrower in scope than Robert's in that it includes only those concerns that the author has learned are most likely to arise at the various levels of local government. Other intentional departures from *Robert's Rules of Order Newly Revised* are justified by statutory provisions or circumstances peculiar to this booklet's intended users. [For example, Robert did not anticipate the constraints imposed by Wisconsin's "Open Meetings Law."] Occasionally, this guide will advise its users to adopt very specific rules of their own when reliance on Robert would not be the best recourse. It is hoped that this simplification and adaptation does not unduly misrepresent the Robert system. Certainly, variance from Robert should not be taken as disrespect for that carefully-wrought and time-honored model of democratic deliberation.

While the spirit of this guide is one of appreciation for members of local units of government and acknowledgment of their sacrifices and service, it does not imply that they bear no responsibility for acquiring at least a rudimentary knowledge of the rules of deliberation that are essential for efficient and fair government decision-making. Specifically, members should:

1. Be aware that there are laws that must be followed in doing the public's business. Higher public law takes precedence over any rules the group may devise for itself and over the rules contained in a manual of procedures such as Robert's.

2. Be familiar with their group's own rules. Units of local government typically have rules of their own expressed in bylaw or ordinance form. Such rules are usually not lengthy or complicated and provide procedures adapted to the particular group's needs.

3. Acquire, as time permits, awareness of the rules contained in standard manuals of procedure as they may apply to the group's deliberations. Consummate skill as a parliamentarian is not a prerequisite to membership in a local unit of government. Nonetheless, an effective member will read through this booklet and will also read, at least selectively, in the manual the group designates as its authority, usually *Robert's Rules of Order Newly Revised*. S/he will learn from those situations in which this guide or the manual is consulted or referred to in resolving questions of procedure. A copy of *Robert's*, or whatever manual is designated, should be available at every meeting.

HOW TO USE THIS BOOKLET

This booklet is most relevant to those situations in which questions of procedure arise that are not resolved by following statutory mandates or any rules the local unit of government itself may have enacted.

In consulting this booklet, locate the issue in question in the "Table of Contents" and then read through the corresponding text and appendices for an explanation.

Every effort has been made to provide direct advice in plain language. As necessary, the booklet will include clarifications in the form of examples and citations of authority. Since different situational paths often lead to the same principle or rule, the reader will encounter redundancy and cross-referencing.

If the particular issue is not clearly resolved in this guide, or seems to be omitted altogether, the next step is to consult *Robert's Rules of Order Newly Revised* or whatever other manual the group may have designated.

The system of parliamentary procedure commonly known as "Robert's Rules of Order" has undergone much revision since its first appearance in 1876. The reader may encounter early versions reissued with very recent publication dates. As of 1998, the most recent and authoritative publication is *Robert's Rules of Order Newly Revised*, published by Addison Wesley Longman, Inc. [Complete bibliographical information is found in the "References" section of this booklet.]

Further guidance may be found in the resources provided by the association that is specific to the level of government or special district involved. As of 1998 such associations include:

League of Wisconsin Municipalities, 202 State Street, Suite 300, Madison, WI, 53703-2215 (267-2380)
Wisconsin Association of School Boards, 122 W. Washington Ave., Madison, WI, 53703 (608-257-2622)
Wisconsin Counties Association, Suite 101, 100 River Place, Monona, WI, 53716-4016 (608-224-5330)

Wisconsin Towns Association, W 7725 State Highway 29, Shawano, WI, 54166 (715-524-3157)

Also helpful is:

Local Government Center, University of Wisconsin-Extension, 610 Langdon St, Madison, WI, 53703 (608-262-9960)

1. RULES FOR GROUP DELIBERATION

Parliamentary procedure is a set of rules designed to protect the rights of participation of members of a group, to insure equal application of those rights, to maintain order, and thereby to protect also the interests of their constituents.

1.1. Some rules of procedure are mandatory for local governments.

1.1.1. All "governmental bodies" in Wisconsin must follow the "Open Meetings Law" [Secs. 19.81 through 19.98 stats.] This law prescribes, among other things, how and when notice for meetings must be issued, what the notice must contain, the circumstances permitting and the procedures for meeting in closed session, and how some votes are to be taken. Relevant portions of the Open Meetings Law will be noted at various points in this booklet. Nonetheless, officials of local government should acquire a familiarity with the law independently of this booklet.

NOTE: An excellent reference is Natkins and Schneider, Understanding Wisconsin's Open Meetings Law. Complete bibliographical information is contained in "References."

1.1.2. All units of local government in Wisconsin are constrained by specific statutory provisions that vary with the unit of government — counties, cities, villages, towns, school and other special districts. These provisions may contain quorum requirements, vote requirements on certain issues and duties and responsibilities of certain officers. Officials of specific levels of local government should become familiar with the statutes that affect them.

1.1.3. Court decisions involving conflicts over procedures may have a bearing on the conduct of the deliberations of local units of government. Such decisions known to be relevant to the precepts contained in this booklet will be noted throughout.

1.2. Local governments may create their own rules within the bounds of higher law.

1.2.1. It is recommended practice for local governments to enact for themselves, in ordinance or bylaw form, rules of procedure specific to their own situation. Such rules typically set forth the regular meeting schedule; procedures to be followed in special or adjourned meetings; quorum requirement; procedures for electing the group's officers; who presides if the chairperson is absent; rules regarding members' attendance; order of business; procedures for putting items on the agenda; rules affecting members' participation in debate; rules affecting manner of voting and requirements for passage of ordinances, resolutions, and other measures; procedures for reconsideration of matters previously voted on; and rules affecting citizen participation.

1.2.2. Such rules as set forth by the unit of local government should specify the subunits (i.e., commissions and committees), if any, to which they apply.

1.2.3. Such rules as set forth by the unit of local government should also include rules that affect the composition and conduct of the group's subunits. In addition to listing the several subunits, such rules should specify the number of members of each subunit and how they are selected, what officers the subunit shall have and how they are to be selected, expectations as to attendance, and grounds for removal (if any).

1.2.4. All rules of procedure passed by local units of government must be within the constraints of statutes and other higher law. The local unit cannot, by passing its own rules, disregard higher law.

NOTE: The League of Wisconsin Municipalities has available sample rules in ordinance form for the conduct of common council and village board meetings. See "References" for specific bibliographical information.

1.3. Local governments may designate a manual of procedure to follow in situations not covered by higher law or their own rules.

1.3.1. Manuals of procedure can provide detail not desired in the group's own rules and can guide in situations not anticipated in the group's own rules.

1.3.2. Although not specifically written for local units of government, the most commonly designated manual for all organizations is *Robert's Rules of Order Newly Revised (herein sometimes referred to as "Robert's," the "Robert's system," or, on occasion, simply "Robert").* The intention here is to be consistent with *Robert's* except in instances in which departures are mandated by higher law or are thought by the author to be advisable on the grounds of clarity and practicality. *(The second most commonly used manual — Sturgis' Standard Code of Parliamentary Procedure — is listed under "References.")*

1.3.3. When the manual designated by the local unit of government contains procedures that are in conflict with higher law or the group's own rules, it is the higher law or the group's own rules — not the manual — that must be followed.

1.4. Local governments may decide on procedures in instances not covered by higher law, their own rules, or their designated manual of procedure.

1.4.1. In situations not covered by higher law, the group's own rules, or the designated manual of procedure, the group may determine for itself, on a case-by-case basis, the procedure(s) to be followed.

1.4.1.1. The chairperson may rule, subject to appeal, as to proper procedure. If appealed, a majority of the members may, by vote, overturn or reject the chair's ruling. A tie vote sustains the chair's ruling. *(See "Appeal from the Decision of the Chair" in Appendix A.)*

1.4.1.2. Rather than ruling in situations where proper procedure is not clearly set forth, the chairperson may submit the proposal as to correct procedure to the members for decision by majority vote.

1.4.1.3. A member may propose a procedure to be used in the particular case. Such motion would need to be passed by a majority of those voting.

1.4.2. Practices once determined and spontaneously adopted on a case-by-case basis may be repeated and thus become expectations. To avoid confusion as to their force as rules, such practices should be examined for their desirability and, if deemed useful, made explicit parts of the group's own rules.

> *NOTE: Practices that are habitual but not clearly grounded in statute, rule, or parliamentary authority, such as allowing citizen input on selected issues, should be explicitly provided for in the group's rules. Otherwise, the group relies on members' recollections and risks confusing and inconsistent procedures. Habitual misapplications such as those stemming from "calling the question" (see 5.8. below) or "friendly amendment" (see 6.9. below) should be prohibited by rule.*

1.5. In certain situations, local governments may suspend their own rules or provisions of their designated manual.

1.5.1. Suspension of the group's own rules must not compromise the rights of constituents or group members, absent or present.

1.5.2. The decision to suspend the rules must be expressly limited as to issue and/or time, and requires unanimous consent or a vote of two-thirds of those voting.

1.5.3. Statutory or other procedures mandated by higher law cannot be suspended by the group.

NOTE: It is common for units of local government to want to expand the opportunity for members of the group or members of the public to speak on certain issues beyond the constraints imposed by their own rules. In such cases, a decision to suspend the rules to enable the specific input would be appropriate if agreed to by unanimous consent or formal motion. Such motion would need to be seconded and passed by 2/3 of the votes cast. (See "Suspend the Rules" in Appendix A.)

2. MEETINGS OF LOCAL GOVERNMENTS

A properly constituted meeting exists when, after reasonable notice has been issued to the members of a group and to the public, a sufficient number of those members come together to do business in the name of the group.

2.1. Local governments must meet regularly.

2.1.1. Local governing bodies are expected to establish a schedule of regular meetings. Such schedule is often a part of their own rules or the ordinances that set forth their procedures.

2.1.2. Some units of local governments — e.g., towns, school districts, other special districts — are required to provide for annual meetings of their constituents. Such annual meetings have fewer and more specific functions than do the meetings of the governing boards.

2.2. "Adjourned meetings" may be arranged.

2.2.1. The members of the group may, during the course of one meeting, set a time to meet again before the next regular meeting in order to complete the current regular meeting's agenda. Such a meeting is called an "adjourned meeting."

2.2.2. An adjourned meeting may be arranged by those members attending even though a quorum is not present. *(See 2.5. below.)*

2.2.3. The agenda of the adjourned meeting will include those items not attended to in the regular meeting and other items that may be added subsequent to the regular meeting.

2.2.4. Under all circumstances, whether new items are added to the adjourned meeting's agenda or not, or whether the adjourned meeting was provided for by fewer than a quorum, the same notice requirements that apply to a regular meeting of the group will apply to the adjourned meeting.

> *EXAMPLE: During the course of a meeting, a snowstorm develops and the members, noting that the remaining items on the agenda are not urgent, decide that it would be prudent to end the current meeting and start for their homes. They also realize that it would be good to attend to the remaining agenda items before the next regular meeting. In this situation, they could, by unanimous consent or by a motion that is made, seconded, and passed by a majority of the votes cast, schedule a meeting of the group for a time prior to the next regular meeting. Similarly, if during the course of a meeting a sufficient number of members leave so that fewer than a quorum is left, those remaining could decide, by unanimous consent or by a formal motion passed by a majority of the votes cast, to schedule a meeting of the entire group for a time prior to the next regular meeting. In either of these cases, public notice of the "adjourned meeting," i.e., the meeting scheduled prior to the next regular meeting, must be issued in the same manner as for any regular meeting of the group. (See discussion of the privileged motion, "set the time to which to adjourn" in Appendix A.)*

2.3. Special or "emergency" meetings may be arranged.

2.3.1. Should an issue requiring prompt attention arise when the group is not in session, or if such an issue that is not on the agenda arises during a meeting, a special or "emergency" meeting may be called to respond to that issue.

2.3.2. It is recommended that the group provide in its own rules that a special or emergency meeting may be called by the chairperson, or the vice-chairperson, or by a specific number of members fewer than a majority.

2.3.3. In the absence of the group's own rules providing for special or emergency meetings, a special meeting may be called by the chairperson of the group or by a majority of the group's members.

2.3.4. If the need to respond to an emergency issue is such that 24 hours public notice is impossible or impractical, the group may meet two hours after public notice has been issued. *[Sec. 19.84(3) stats.] (Also, see 2.4.4.1. below.)*

2.4. Notice of meetings must be provided to all members and to the public.

2.4.1. Notice that a meeting is to take place must set forth the time, place, and business to be conducted at the meeting.

2.4.1.1. A description of business to be conducted must be sufficiently specific to inform an interested party of the issues to be discussed or the decisions that may be made. General categories such as "reports," "unfinished business," "new business" or "other matters that may come before the body" are insufficient.

2.4.2. If a notice of a meeting is distributed to members, such notice must be distributed to all members.

> *NOTE: Practice varies in that some groups issue notice of a meeting to the members, while other groups simply assume that members will be aware of the schedule of meetings. If notice is issued to members, care must be taken to ensure that all members receive the meeting notice and any accompanying background materials.*

2.4.3. The responsibility for issuing notice to members is that it be reasonably posted or distributed, but not that it be received.

2.4.4. Notice to the public must conform to the requirements of Wisconsin's Open Meetings Law. Notice to the public includes both posting notices and informing interested media.

2.4.4.1. The statutes currently require 24-hours notice to the public of a regular meeting. If, for "good cause," such notice is impossible or impractical to issue, a shorter notice period may be given provided it is not less that two hours. *[Sec. 19.84(3) stats.]*

> *NOTE: As a practical matter, it is advisable for the clerk to keep a record of when meeting notices are made public.*

2.5. A quorum of the members must be present to do business in the name of the group.

2.5.1. A quorum is the minimum number of members or proportion of the membership that must be present to do business in the name of the group.

2.5.1.1 If fewer members than a quorum are present, business done or decisions made are not binding on the group.

2.5.1.2. Personal liability may be incurred by members who number fewer than a quorum but who act or decide as though for the group.

2.5.2. The group may set its own quorum threshold but may not provide that fewer than a majority of the members may constitute a quorum.

> *NOTE: In private sector organizations, particularly those with a large number of members and geographical diversity, it is common to provide that a proportion of members less than a majority may constitute a quorum. In public bodies, however, at least a majority of the members must be present to constitute a quorum. Indeed, public bodies' own rules often require that more than a majority of the membership must be present to constitute a quorum.*

2.5.3. If the group's quorum is not expressed in statute or group's rule, the quorum requirement is a majority of the members.

2.5.4. The quorum requirement for groups with a specified number of members is not reduced in the event of vacant seats in the membership.

2.5.5. A member who has a conflict of interest on a particular issue is not included as part of the quorum for the deliberations on that issue. Thus, while a quorum may otherwise be present at the meeting, the fact of a member in conflict on a particular issue may prevent action on that issue by reason of a lack of quorum.

> *EXAMPLE: Suppose a group has a total of 11 members and its rules specify that a majority of them be present to constitute a quorum. At a given meeting, 6 of the 11 are present, thus the quorum threshold is satisfied. However, on a given issue, one of the members has a conflict of interest. Thus, for that issue, there are not enough qualified voters present to constitute a quorum. In this circumstance, that issue cannot be acted on in this meeting unless another member who is not in conflict arrives. Other issues, assuming no conflicts, may be deliberated and decided.*

2.5.6. When exercising the powers of the governing body, as when voting on resolutions or ordinances (as opposed to making procedural decisions) a number of members equal to a quorum must vote. If abstentions, due to conflicts or otherwise, reduce the total number of votes cast to fewer than the number of members required for a quorum, the measure cannot pass.

> *EXAMPLE: The Wisconsin Supreme Court in Board of Supervisors of Oconto County v. Hall, 47 Wis. 208, 2 N.W.291 (1879) held that a quorum must vote. The situation giving rise to the court case was similar to the example above, in that a conflict of interest dictated that a member abstain from voting, thus reducing the number of qualified voters to fewer than a quorum. It would appear, however, that members abstaining for any reason — whether in conflict or not — could reduce the number of votes cast to fewer than the quorum requirement, thus precluding action on the issue.*

2.5.7. The requirement that "a quorum must vote" does not necessarily mean that a majority of the total membership must favor the proposed action. The exact number or proportion of votes required to pass the measure is situation-specific. *(See 7.7 below.)*

2.5.8. A gathering of members numbering fewer than a quorum at a duly noticed meeting may take action to compel the attendance of absent members *(see 2.6.)* or may provide for an adjourned meeting *(see 2.2.)*.

2.5.9. A gathering of members numbering fewer than quorum but of sufficient number to block passage of a contemplated action (a "negative quorum") may be a violation of the Open Meetings Law.

> *NOTE: The "Open Meetings Law" provides that a gathering of half the members of a body satisfies the numbers test to determine if a meeting is being held. In the Showers Case, [State ex rel. Newspapers, Inc. v. Showers, 135 Wis. 2d 77, 398 W. 2d 154 (1987)] this principle was extended by noting that a gathering of a number of members fewer than half would similarly satisfy the test of numbers if there were enough of them to block passage on a particular issue that required more than a simple majority of the votes cast for passage.*

2.5.10. A series of gatherings or conferences, in person or electronically, of members numbering fewer than a quorum but of sufficient number, taken in the aggregate across such gatherings, to control the outcome of an anticipated measure or proposal (a "walking quorum") may be a violation of the Open Meetings Law if the exchanges of information or opinion relate to the anticipated measure.

2.6. Members may be required to attend meetings.

2.6.1. Units of local government may direct law enforcement officers to locate absent members and bring them to the meeting.

2.6.2. A group may specify in its own rules the grounds and procedures for granting excused absences and the penalties for unexcused absences.

2.7. Presence in the same room constitutes attendance.

2.7.1. As long as a member is in the room where a meeting is being held, s/he is regarded as being in attendance.

2.7.2. Should a member leave his/her seat or station, but remain in the meeting room, such departure from the seat or station does not constitute an absence that might affect the presence of a quorum. If a member does not respond to a vote taken while the member is away from his/her seat but is still in the room, the member is regarded as having abstained.

EXAMPLE: Mason relates an instance in which six members of a school board in Indiana met to select a new superintendent. There were two candidates and, after repeated voting, the members remained deadlocked with three of them favoring each candidate. At one point, the three members favoring one of the candidates, apparently frustrated with the lack of progress, left the table around which the members were meeting and started visiting with the onlookers. The chairperson, who remained at the meeting table, called for another vote, the outcome of which was 3-0 in favor of one candidate. The contract was awarded to the winning candidate but the losing faction sought to block the action in court by claiming that when they left the meeting table, they had de facto *left the meeting, and, therefore, there was no quorum at the meeting. The court ruled that, as long as they remained in the room, they had not left the meeting. Their non-responses to the vote were regarded as abstentions. [Paul Mason, "The Legal Side of Parliamentary Procedure."* Today's Speech. *Vol. IV, No. 4 (Nov. 1956, p. 11)]*
NOTE: The concept that "a quorum must vote" that the Wisconsin Supreme Court observed in Board of Supervisors of Oconto County v. Hall, *47 Wis. 208, 2 N.W. 291 (1879), apparently was not noted in this decision.*

2.8. Teleconference participation in meetings may be permitted.

2.8.1. A group meeting by teleconference, or including an otherwise absent member via speakerphone, may be permitted if the public's right to monitor the proceedings is not compromised.

2.8.2. Meeting by teleconference or including absent members by teleconference that does not enable the public or the media to monitor the meeting effectively may violate the Open Meetings Law.

NOTE: There are many factors that may make meetings that are conducted wholly or partly by teleconference qualitatively different than face-to-face meetings. Teleconference meetings should be conducted only when clearly warranted by circumstance, and never simply for convenience.

2.9. Meetings of local governments may be held in closed session under specific, limited circumstances.

2.9.1. Wisconsin's Open Meetings Law provides that "...all meetings of all state and local governments shall be publicly held in places reasonably accessible to members of the public and shall be open to all citizens at all times unless otherwise expressly provided by law." [*Sec. 19.81(2) stats.]*

2.9.2. While meeting in closed session may be permitted to deliberate on specific issues, **meeting in closed session is never required**.

2.9.3. Convening a meeting of a local government body in closed session is permitted only for the purposes specified in Wisconsin's Open Meetings Law secs.19.851(a)-(j).

NOTE: For a full explanation of the purposes for which a local government may convene in closed session, and the specific requirements for meeting notices and procedures, see Natkins and Schneider, Understanding Wisconsin's Open Meetings Law. (Bibliographical information contained in "References.")

3. USING THE AGENDA

The agenda for a meeting creates expectations for members and the public as to the items of business that will be taken up and the order in which they will be considered; once set, the agenda may be changed only in limited ways.

3.1. The chairperson is responsible for the agenda.

3.1.1. Although other personnel, such as hired staff, may do the physical work in preparing an agenda, the chairperson of the group is ultimately responsible for the agenda's content, distribution, and use.

3.1.2. Any matter known to the chairperson as likely to become subject matter for the meeting should be included on the agenda.

3.2. A specific agenda is the best form of meeting notice.

3.2.1. Public bodies are required to issue specific notice of the subject matter of the meeting to the public.

3.2.2. Although notice in the form of an agenda is not required, an agenda that sets forth the several topics to be covered, and in what sequence, is the best form of notice.

3.2.3. An agenda that is made up only of general categories is insufficient.

3.2.3.1. Headings such as "reports," "unfinished business" or "new business" are not sufficient to advise the members or the public of the subject matter of the meeting.

3.3. If necessary, new items can be added to the agenda prior to the meeting if timely public notice of the additions can be provided.

3.3.1. If it becomes necessary to add items to an agenda that has already been made public, such additions must be announced and posted as soon as possible, and in no case less than two hours prior to the meeting.

> *NOTE: The minimum notice requirement of 24 hours for public notice would apply to any addition to the agenda unless for "good cause" it was impossible or impractical to do so, in which case the group may meet no sooner than 2 hours after issuing public notice. [Sec. 19.84(3) stats.] (Also, see 2.4.4.2. above.)*

3.4. Members of the group must have a reasonable opportunity to place matters on the agenda.

3.4.1. The group's own rules should specify the procedures for individual members to contribute items to the agenda of an upcoming meeting.

3.4.2. During a meeting, members can, by group action, order that items not on the present meeting's agenda be placed on the agenda of a specific future meeting.

3.4.3. Once an item on the present meeting's agenda becomes pending, the group can postpone it to a specific future meeting, in which case it must appear on that future meeting's agenda.

3.4.4. An item on the agenda and pending in one meeting may be referred to a committee charged with considering the matter and reporting its findings at a specific future meeting. In this case, the item would appear under "committee reports" on the future meeting's agenda.

> *NOTE: When the group orders that items be placed on a specific future meeting's agenda, it is, in parliamentary procedure terms, creating an "order of the day" for that meeting. In fact, the group may also specify the time the ordered matter is to be taken up or its placement on the agenda of the future meeting. An "order of the day" must be honored — the agenda-setter has no choice but to put the matter on the agenda as ordered. In non-public bodies, a member noticing that the ordered item is not on the agenda may "call for the orders of the day" thus bringing the neglected matter before the group at the proper time. However, units of local government in Wisconsin must take into account the constraints imposed by the Open Meetings Law. Assuming that the neglected matter was not on the public notice for the meeting, a call for the orders of the day cannot bring the matter before the group until proper public notice is issued. If the omission cannot be remedied before the future meeting begins by amending the notice in timely manner, the group may have to create a special meeting with the two-hours notice period as required by law. (See "Special or 'emergency' meetings may be arranged" in 2.3. above and the discussion of the privileged motion, "call for the orders of the day," in Appendix A.)*

3.5. The order in which items on the agenda are taken up for consideration may be changed by 2/3 of the members voting.

3.5.1. Once set and announced, the agenda for a meeting becomes an expectation with the force of a rule for that meeting. To change the expectation, i.e., to "suspend the rule," requires the agreement of at least 2/3 of those voting. *(See the discussion of the incidental motion, "suspend the rules," in Appendix A.)*

3.6. New items may not be added to the agenda for action later in

the same meeting.

3.6.1. Items other than those on the announced agenda for a given meeting may arise spontaneously during discussion or through citizen input. Such items may not be acted on during the meeting in which they arise.

3.6.2. The group may receive information from members of the public during public comment segments of the agenda but may not act on any matter thus arising during the meeting unless the matter was included in the meeting's notice. The group may place such items on a future agenda (i.e., "order" that the matter be taken up at a future meeting).

3.7. New items added to the agenda of an adjourned meeting must be included in the notice of the adjourned meeting.

3.7.1. If an adjourned meeting is provided for as described in 2.2 above, the notice of the adjourned meeting must include any items added that were not on the original meeting's agenda as well as "carry-over" items from the original meeting.

3.8. "Carry-over" items from previous meetings must be specifically identified on the agenda.

3.8.1. Items that were on the previous meeting's agenda but not attended to when the meeting adjourned, items postponed by group action to the current meeting, and items referred to a committee for consideration and report to the current meeting must be specifically listed on the agenda for the current meeting. Listing merely a heading such as "unfinished business" is insufficient.

3.8.2. Items that may be reconsidered during a meeting must be on the meeting's agenda. If a decision is made to reconsider an item not on the agenda, the reconsideration must be delayed to a future meeting so that proper notice can be issued. *(See the discussion of the motion to "reconsider" in Appendix A.)*

3.8.3. Items may not be "taken from the table" and deliberated unless the item is on the agenda. An item may be taken from the table and scheduled for deliberation at a future meeting. *(See discussion of the motion "take from the table" in Appendix A.)*

3.8.4. If the chairperson or a member knows that a motion to reconsider or to take an item from the table is likely to occur, the agenda and notice should so indicate.

EXAMPLE: The agenda could state "Possible motion to reconsider...," or "Possible motion to take from the table the tabled motion to...."

3.9. A time-specific agenda item must be taken up at the time indicated on the notice and agenda unless two-thirds of the members agree to take it up at a different time.

3.9.1. The agenda, once set, has the force of a rule. A decision to alter the agenda may be made by unanimous consent or by a vote of at least two-thirds of the votes cast. *(See the incidental motion to "suspend the rules" in Appendix A.)*

3.10. The times during a meeting that are set aside for public input should be clearly identified on the agenda.

3.10.1. Public input may be invited on particular items.

3.10.2. Public input may be invited at a particular time during the meeting on any item on the agenda.

3.10.3. Time may be set aside for the public to provide input on any matter of concern to them whether on the meeting's agenda or not. However, any item so arising that is not on the meeting's agenda may not be acted on by the group except to decide to put it on a future meeting's agenda. The group may, however, receive information on the item from members of the public.

NOTE: See 5.9. below for a more complete discussion of procedures for citizen participation.

4. THE ROLE AND AUTHORITY OF THE CHAIR

> ***If the chairperson is a member of the group, s/he has the same rights of participation as any other member, although the exercise of those rights may be restricted while the chairperson is presiding.***

4.1. If the chairperson is a member of the group, s/he has all the rights of participation as any other member.

4.1.1. The rights of participation are the right to make and second motions, the right to enter into discussion and debate, and the right to vote.

4.1.2. In Wisconsin, **Mayors** preside over Common Councils but are not members of the same stature as alderpersons. Mayors are not counted in determining the presence of a quorum and their rights of participation are restricted, in part, by statute. ***The status of mayors as participants will be noted in the sections below.***

4.2. The chairperson's right to vote, if s/he is a member of the group, may not be abridged, except in the case of a conflict of interest, whether or not s/he is presiding at the time of the vote.

4.2.1. While the chairperson may choose to abstain from voting at any time, a unit of local government may not —by rule or otherwise— restrict a member-chairperson who is not in conflict to voting only in specific situations such as when the outcome of the vote is tied.

4.2.2. A member-chairperson, at his/her own volition, may choose to exercise his/her right to vote only in cases in which the chair's vote would affect the outcome. Under this practice, the chairperson, favoring a measure, would vote in the affirmative when his/her vote would create the majority or other proportion needed for passage. In this situation, the chairperson who opposes the measure could, but need not, vote in the negative since the measure would be lost regardless of his/her vote. Further under this practice, a member-chairperson who opposes a measure could vote in the negative if the inclusion of his/her vote would deny the majority or other proportion needed for passage. Thus, if the measure would otherwise pass by a one-vote margin, the chairperson could vote in the negative, thus creating a tie, thereby defeating the proposal. In this situation, the chairperson who favors passage could, but need not, vote in the affirmative. The measure would pass regardless.

> *EXAMPLE: (The following anecdote illustrating a misunderstanding of the chairperson's right to vote has been slightly fictionalized but is based on an actual occurrence.) A city's Historical Landmark Commission was voting on a proposal to remove a particular structure from the list of protected buildings. The vote was 4 - 3 in favor of removal. The chairperson did not vote. Afterward the chairperson announced that she was not in favor of removing the structure from the list but, since the vote was not tied, she could not vote. Had the chairperson known what her options actually were, she could have voted in the negative, creating a tie, thus defeating the measure.*

4.2.3. The chairperson should not refrain from voting simply because s/he presides over the meeting. For the chairperson to refrain from voting unless his/her vote will alter the outcome may have the advantage in that it promotes an appearance of impartiality, but such advantage may be offset in that it denies constituents knowledge of the chairperson's position. A chairperson elected from a particular district, such as a county board chairperson, leaves his/her constituents unrepresented if s/he does not vote. The recommended practice is for the chairperson to assume that s/he will vote on every issue and to refrain from voting only when in conflict of interest or when the need to achieve a stance of impartiality is particularly pressing. Again, the member-chairperson who does not have a conflict of interest has the **right** to vote whenever s/he so desires.

4.2.4. **Mayors** of cities, who preside over Common Council meetings, are not regarded as members of the Council as far as voting rights are concerned. Statutes restrict the mayor's right to vote to cases in which there is a tie vote among the Council.

4.2.4.1. **Mayors** may vote, but need not, when the Council votes are tied. If the Mayor opposes the measure, s/he need not vote in the negative. The measure will fail regardless.

4.2.4.2. **Mayors** may **not** vote in the negative to create a tie or otherwise deny the proportion required for passage. If a measure is favored by a sufficient proportion of the Council to enable passage, the Mayor may block passage by use of his/her veto authority, which, in turn, may be overridden by a 2/3 vote of the full Council.

4.3. The member-chairperson's right to participate in deliberations by making or seconding motions or entering into the discussion may not be abridged but s/he may be required to vacate the chair to exercise those rights.

4.3.1. While the member-chairperson may choose not to participate in deliberations while presiding, s/he has the right to do so unless the group by rule or otherwise instructs the chairperson to vacate the chair for such purposes.

4.3.2. The chairperson may vacate the chair for purposes of deliberating by turning the responsibilities of presiding over to another who is acceptable to the group.

4.3.2.1. The elected vice-chairperson usually assumes the vacated chair.

4.3.2.2. If there is no elected vice-chairperson, any other member acceptable to the group may preside over the deliberations.

4.3.3. In small units of local government, the chairperson may assume the right to participate in deliberations while occupying the chair.

4.3.3.1. If a group believes a chair's participation in the deliberations interferes with his/her role as presider, they may order the chair to vacate in order to participate.

4.3.3.2. A group may not require that a chairperson remain in the chair and also refrain from participation. The chairperson must be provided the option of vacating to participate if the group does not want the chairperson to participate while presiding.

4.3.4. When any chairperson vacates the chair for purposes of participation, s/he must abide by all rules of discussion and debate that apply to other members.

4.3.5. Once a chairperson has vacated the chair, either voluntarily or upon the order of the group, s/he may not return to chair until the issue under deliberation is no longer pending.

4.3.6. In the case of **mayors**, the recommended practice is to get consent from the council before participating in discussion or making or seconding motions.

> *NOTE: City councils should stipulate in their own rules of procedure the desired constraints governing the mayor's participation so that such concerns don't become matters of contention in specific situations.*

4.3.6.1. If a mayor vacates, the president of the council presides over the deliberations on the pending issue.

4.3.6.2. If a mayor vacates, the rules in 4.3.4. and 4.3.5. above apply.

4.4. The chairperson is responsible for administering the group's deliberations.

4.4.1. The chairperson is the gatekeeper of ideas coming before the group.

4.4.1.1. The chairperson oversees the agenda-setting process.

4.4.1.2. The chairperson announces the issue before the group and requires that members' remarks be relevant to the issue.

4.4.1.3. When a motion is made and seconded, the chairperson states it for clarity, thus making it the pending matter of business.

4.4.2. The chairperson regulates members' participation in the deliberations.

4.4.2.1. The chairperson recognizes members who wish to participate in the discussion. While such recognition may not be necessary in informal contexts, the chairperson has the authority to require it when s/he sees fit.

4.4.2.2. The chairperson is expected to seek balance in the debate.

4.4.2.3. The chairperson is expected to keep members' remarks relevant to the issue at hand.

4.4.2.4. The chairperson enforces the group's rules governing debate, including any rules of decorum the group may have.

4.4.3. The chairperson conducts the decision-making process.

4.4.3.1. The chairperson is expected to make it clear to the group when a decision is being made, whether the decision is by voting or by unanimous consent.

> *EXAMPLE: Mason reports the case of the minister in Ohio who sought a salary increase from his church's governing board. Although each member of the board expressed that granting the raise would be a fine thing, no formal vote was taken. When no salary increase came about, the minister complained in court that the board was going back on its agreement. The court disagreed. In the absence of a formal record that a decision was made, there was no evidence that the board had, in fact, agreed to the raise. Chairpersons must make it clear, both at the time and in the record, that a decision is being made. [Paul Mason, "The Legal Side of Parliamentary Procedure," Today's Speech, Vol. IV, No. 4 (Nov. 1956, p. 11)]*

4.4.3.2. When votes are taken by voice or in a visible form such as raising hands, the chairperson must ask for the votes on each side. Regardless of how one-sided the outcome may seem after affirmative votes are taken, negative votes must always be called for.

4.4.3.3. The chairperson announces the outcome of the voting. When voting is conducted in a counted form, the number of votes cast on each side of the issue is announced.

4.4.3.4. When voting is by voice only, the chairperson's announcement of the outcome is subject to a request for a "division of the assembly," which may be called for by any member. A "division of the assembly" requires that the vote be retaken in a visible form. A member wishing a division of the assembly must call for it immediately after the chair announces the results of the voice vote and before any additional business transpires. *(See discussion of the incidental motion "call for a division of the assembly" in Appendix A.)*

4.5. The chairperson is obliged to respond to members' reasonable requests and inquiries.

4.5.1. Any member is entitled to request and/or make inquiries regarding virtually anything s/he wants that is relevant to the situation, including substantive information on the issue, advice as to proper procedure, or provisions for personal comfort. *(See Appendix A for a discussion of the privileged motion "raise a question of privilege" and the incidental motion "parliamentary inquiry.")*

4.5.2. The chairperson is obliged to respond to each request or inquiry as fully as possible, provided the interests of the group as a whole are not unduly compromised.

4.5.3. If a chairperson cannot provide the information or grant a member's request, or believes it is not in the group's interests to do so, an explanation to that effect is required.

4.5.4. If a member believes the chairperson's response to an inquiry or request is inadequate, s/he may "appeal from the decision of the chair." The appeal, if seconded, leads to a vote as to whether or not to alter the chair's decision. A majority of those voting would be required to uphold the appeal and change the decision.

EXAMPLE: During the course of a meeting, a member believes the group would profit from reviewing background material that was distributed in written form at the previous meeting. Unfortunately, none of the members nor the clerk has the material with them at the current meeting. The member requests that the chairperson direct the clerk to return to the office and duplicate the material for redistribution at the current meeting. The chairperson doubts that the usefulness of the material warrants the disruption and inconvenience and responds, in effect, that s/he believes the group can proceed without the background material. The member honestly believes the chairperson is wrong and appeals from the decision. The matter is then put to the group to determine whether the chairperson's decision is to be overturned and the clerk is to be sent for the materials. A majority of those voting would have to vote to overturn the decision; a tie vote would sustain the decision. (See the discussion on the incidental motion, "Appeal from the Decision of the Chair," in Appendix A.)

4.6. The chairperson must rule on points of order.

4.6.1. If a member believes that any of the group's rules or the rules of its chosen manual of authority are being violated, s/he may raise a "point of order." After hearing the member's "point," the chairperson must rule as to whether the member is correct and changes in procedure are warranted.

EXAMPLE: Suppose the group's own rules provide that no member may be recognized to speak a second time on a particular issue if someone who has not yet spoken is seeking recognition. The chairperson, inadvertently perhaps, recognizes a member to speak a second time instead of a member seeking recognition for the first time. Any member could then interrupt the proceedings by saying "point of order" (or some such language). The chair is obliged to ask the basis for the point of order and then respond by correcting the error or by stating why s/he believes no procedural error has been made. (See the discussion of the incidental motion, "Point of Order," in Appendix A.)

4.6.2. If a member believes that the chairperson's ruling is incorrect, s/he may "appeal from the decision of the chair," thus initiating the process described in the example following 4.5.4. above.

4.7. The chairperson is responsible for notices and agendas of meetings.

4.7.1. Although specific tasks in issuing notice and setting the agenda may be assigned to others, the chairperson is ultimately responsible for the proper issuance of notice and timely distribution of the agenda.

4.7.2. The chairperson is responsible for assuring members reasonable access to the agenda-setting process in accordance with the group's own rules.

4.7.3. The chairperson ensures that items ordered to be taken up at a particular meeting are on the notice and agenda. *(See 3.4. above.)*

4.7.4. The chairperson ensures that the agenda, once set, is followed unless the group orders changes in the order in which topics are taken up. *(See 3.5. above.)*

4.7.5. If a member notes that items ordered for the current meeting are not on the agenda, or if the expected agenda is not followed, s/he may "call for the orders of the day," which requires the chair to correct the situation in a reasonable and equitable manner or explain that the member is wrong and that the agenda has been properly set and is being followed. *(See discussion of the privileged motion, "Call for the Orders of the Day," in Appendix A.)*

4.7.5.1. If the member believes the chairperson to be incorrect in explaining that the agenda has been properly set and/or is being followed, s/he may "appeal from the decision of the chair," thus initiating the process described in the example following 4.5.4. above.

4.7.5.2. If an item ordered for the current meeting is not on the agenda and a member points this out (*de facto* calling for the orders of the day), the item cannot be considered in the current meeting if it was not included in the notice of the meeting. In such case, the item would be ordered for the next meeting or, if deemed important enough, could be made the business of an adjourned or special meeting.

4.8. The chairperson oversees committees and is often, *ex officio*, a member of a committee.

4.8.1. Unless someone else is specifically designated to do so, the chairperson is the liaison between the group and all of its committees.

4.8.2. The group's own rules may designate the chairperson as an *ex officio* member of one or more of the group's committees.

4.8.2.1. "*Ex officio*" membership on a committee or other body means that the individual is a member of the body because of his/her "office." It does not mean "unofficial."

4.8.2.2. Unless otherwise expressed in statute or organizational rule applicable to the particular case, the chairperson as an *ex officio* member of a committee has all the rights of participation as any other member, but does not have the responsibility to attend. Thus, s/he may make and second motions, enter into discussion and debate, and vote, but is not counted in determining whether a quorum is present.

4.8.3. The chairperson does not have the automatic right to appoint members of a committee. Such right must be extended by statute or organizational rule. If there is no explicit delegation of the right to appoint committees, the determination of committee membership is done by the group. The group may delegate the appointment of members of committees to the chairperson on a case-by-case basis.

4.9. The chairperson is generally regarded as the spokesperson for the group.

4.9.1. Unless someone else is specifically identified to do so, the chairperson is the main liaison between the group and the general public and other outside groups.

4.9.2. The chairperson, or any spokesperson for the group, must be careful to separate his/her own opinions from those of the group.

5. RULES OF DISCUSSION AND DEBATE

Democratic decision-making requires fair and equal opportunities for all members to participate in deliberations.

5.1. The rules of discussion and debate may apply whether or not a motion is pending.

5.1.1. There may be discussion of a general issue even though no motion is pending. If so, any rules pertaining to recognition, time limits on speeches, or other considerations of discussion and debate may be applied by the chairperson.

NOTE: Many people think that Robert categorically prohibits discussion on an issue if there is no motion pending. While such prohibition is recommended for large groups like conventions of delegates, Robert advises that in small boards "Informal discussion of a subject is permitted while no motion is pending." [p. 478]

5.2. The rules of discussion and debate are administered by the chairperson, subject to appeal. *(See 4.4. above.)*

5.2.1. Recognizing members who wish to speak, enforcing time limits on speakers, and administering any other rules of discussion and debate the group may have are "rulings" of the chair.

5.2.2. A member who believes the chair is unfair or incorrect in enforcing the rules of discussion and debate may appeal the chair's "ruling." If the appeal is seconded, a majority of the members can overturn the chairperson's ruling. *(See Appendix A for a discussion of the privileged motion, "appeal from the decision of the chair.")*

5.2.3. The chairperson may choose to relax the rules of debate as long as fair play prevails and no one's rights are violated. However, any member may insist that any expressed rules be observed.

> *NOTE: It is recommended that the group expresses its own rules such as those regarding time limits on members' contributions or the number of times a member may speak on a given issue.*

5.3. A member may need to be recognized by the chair to participate in discussion and debate.

5.3.1. Whether provided for in the group's own rules or not, the chairperson may require that members be recognized prior to speaking in discussion and debate.

5.3.2. The requirement that members be recognized by the chair prior to speaking may be relaxed at the discretion of the chair unless a member insists that the recognition requirement be applied to all members during the course of the discussion of a particular issue.

5.3.3. The recognition requirement notwithstanding, a member may interrupt another who is speaking in order to raise a point of order or make inquiries or requests of immediate concern. *(See Appendix A for a discussion of the privileged motions "call for the orders of the day" and "raise a question of privilege," and the incidental motions "parliamentary inquiry," "request for information," "point of order," "division of the assembly," "appeal from the decision of the chair," and "object to consideration.")*

5.4. Comments made in discussion and debate must be topically relevant.

5.4.1. When a motion is pending before the group, the discussion and debate must be relevant to the specific action proposed by the motion.

5.4.2. When an issue is discussed but no motion is pending, comments must be relevant to the subject matter of the issue under discussion.

5.4.3. The chairperson may rule that contributions that are not relevant to the motion or to the subject before the group are out of order. Such rulings are subject to appeal. *(See Appendix A for a discussion of the incidental motion, "appeal from the decision of the chair.")*

5.4.4. The chairperson may enforce any rules of decorum the group may have and, in the absence of specific rules, should, as needed, caution members against hostile and/or personally vindictive remarks.

5.5. Comments made in discussion and debate may be limited as to length.

5.5.1. Whether provided for in the group's own rules or not, the chairperson may rule that a member must bring his/her contribution to a close within a reasonable time. Such ruling is subject to appeal.

5.5.2. The group may establish rules on a case-by-case basis that limit the total time spent on discussion and debate on a particular issue, the number of times a member may speak on the issue, and/or the length of each comment made on the issue. *(See Appendix A for a discussion of the incidental motion, "limit or extend debate.")*

5.5.3. It is recommended that the group's own rules provide desirable limitations on the length and/or number of contributions of members and nonmembers when they are invited to participate. Any such provisions may be suspended by unanimous consent or two-thirds of the members voting. *(See Appendix A for a discussion of the incidental motion, "suspend the rules.")*

5.6. Equal opportunity to participate must be extended to all positions on an issue.

5.6.1. The chairperson is expected to recognize all those who wish to participate without regard to their positions on the issue. If a member believes that the chair is systematically not recognizing certain member(s), s/he may appeal the chair's "ruling" (i.e., deciding whom to recognize) as in 5.2.2.

5.6.2. To avoid the appearance of favoritism in administering debate, it is advisable that the chairperson seek balanced participation from the various positions on the issue.

5.6.3. To avoid the appearance of favoritism in administering debate, it is advisable that the chairperson recognize a member who has not yet spoken on the issue before recognizing a member who has already spoken.

5.7. Conflicts of interest must be disclosed.

5.7.1. A member who knows s/he may gain in a personal or pecuniary way from the outcome of a decision should make that possibility known.

5.7.2. Members who will receive personal or pecuniary gain from the outcome of a decision may not vote on that issue.

5.7.3. Members who have disclosed a potential or actual conflict of interest should be allowed to represent constituents by participating in discussion and debate.

> *NOTE: Members of local government bodies might review section 946.13 stats making it a felony to have a personal pecuniary interest in certain business of the governmental body. A discussion of these conflicts is beyond the purpose of this booklet.*

5.7.4. The abstention of a member in conflict of interest may result in fewer than a quorum voting, thus precluding passing the measure at hand. *(See 2.5.4., 2.5.6. and 2.5.7.)*

5.8. The group may decide to close discussion and debate.

5.8.1. The group may decide by two-thirds vote or unanimous consent to close discussion and debate on the pending issue.

5.8.2. "Calling the question" by a single member does not, in and of itself, require that the discussion and debate on an issue be closed.

5.8.3. The chairperson may regard a single member's "call for the question" as a request and ask if the group is ready to vote on the pending issue. If, however, any other member desires that the discussion and debate continue, discussion and debate can only be closed by a formal motion to close debate. Such motion requires a second and an affirmative vote of two-thirds of those voting to pass. *(See Appendix A for a discussion of the subsidiary motion, "close debate." This motion is called "move the previous question" in the Robert system.)*

5.8.4. The motion to close debate ("previous question") is out of order as long as any member who has not yet spoken on the issue is seeking recognition.

> *CLARIFICATION: Section 5.8.4. is best understood as the opinion of the author. Robert, in discussing procedure in small boards, says, "...motions to close or limit debate generally should not be entertained." (p.478). It would indeed be undesirable, especially in public bodies, to enable even a sizable majority to deny others the right to speak in debate. On the other hand, a group with no rules of its own to govern debate may legitimately want to preclude a filibuster by a small minority. One solution is the position expressed in 5.8.4. A group that agrees that 5.8.4. is a good procedure should incorporate it into its own rules.*

5.9. The group's own rules may provide for citizen participation during a meeting.

5.9.1. Wisconsin's Open Meetings Law provides that citizens have the right to attend and observe meetings of local government units except in very limited circumstances. Such provision, however, does not give them the right to participate.

5.9.2. Citizen participation in the meeting is out of order unless the group, by rule or by decision in a specific situation, extends the right to participate.

5.9.3. Local government units should establish rules governing citizen participation in their meetings. Such rules would apply to the business meetings of the group itself, but not to mandated hearings or to the annual meetings of towns and school and other special districts.

5.9.4. The group's rules may provide for a time on the agenda for general citizen comment to the group.

5.9.4.1. Citizen comments should be primarily one-way, from the citizen to the group. Responses from members of the group should be limited to seeking information or acknowledging that the citizen has been understood. It is out of order for a group member to debate with a citizen or for the group to take action on the citizen's concern at that time. The group may agree that the concern will be put on a future agenda. *(See 3.6.)*

5.9.4.2. The time allotted to a citizen for input should be limited by rule. Clarifying questions from the group are not included in the citizen's speaking time.

5.9.5. The group's rules may provide for citizen comment on a specific issue.

5.9.5.1. The group may set aside time within any agenda item for citizens to comment on that item.

5.9.5.2. The rules at 5.9.4. regarding group members' response to citizen comment will apply in this provision.

5.10. Rules of discussion and debate may be suspended.

5.10.1. Any expressed rule in the group's own rules or its designated manual of procedure that limits or otherwise regulates discussion and debate may be suspended by decision of the group.

5.10.1.2. The decision to suspend the rules may be made by unanimous consent or, if a vote is needed, by two-thirds of those voting. *(See Appendix A for a discussion of the incidental motion, "suspend the rules.")*

5.10.2. Any statutory regulation limiting or otherwise regulating discussion and debate may not be suspended by the group.

5.10.3. Any suggestion or formal motion that a rule be suspended should be specific as to the rule being suspended, the reason for doing so, and the intended duration of the suspension.

> *EXAMPLE: Suppose a group had a rule providing that a member may not speak more than twice on any pending motion. However, on one particular motion, Member X is particularly knowledgeable. The group may, by unanimous consent or by a motion to "suspend the rules," permit Member X to speak any number of times on the pending motion. One way to express the motion properly would be, "I move to suspend the rule that limits the number of times a member may speak on a pending motion so that Member X may speak as many times as s/he desires while the current motion is pending."*

5.11. Some procedural motions may not be debatable.

5.11.1. The Robert's system provides that some procedural motions are undebatable when to debate the motion would be contrary to the motion's intent.

5.11.1.1. The undebatability of a motion does not preclude discussion to clarify the motion's intent and effect. (*See the chart in Appendix B for a listing of motions that are not debatable.)*

6. RULES RELATING TO MOTIONS

Motions are formal proposals that bring substantive or procedural business before the group for discussion and decision.

6.1. Motions are required for substantive matters of business.

6.1.1. "Substantive" matters are official actions of the group as it makes decisions in the form of ordinances and resolutions that affect the community it serves.

6.1.1.2. While some procedural issues may be decided by unanimous consent, official, "substantive" matters should be decided by the formal motion process.

6.2. "Negative" motions should be avoided if at all possible.

6.2.1. Motions typically propose that the group take a particular action and, if voted down, the group does not take the action. If a motion is worded in the negative, i.e., that the group not take an action, it does not follow that the defeat of the motion requires the group to take the action. Ordinarily, to avoid ambiguity, motions expressed in the negative should be ruled out of order and every effort made to express the motion in the affirmative.

6.2.2. In the event that an affirmative statement of the motion cannot be agreed to, and the negative motion is stated by the chairperson, members should be made aware of the effect of voting down the negative motion.

> *EXAMPLE: A village board is discussing, informally without a pending motion, whether to pay the expenses of the village president to attend a seminar on land use planning. During the discussion, a member moves that "the board not pay the expenses of the president to attend the land use planning seminar." If this motion is eventually voted down, the board is left with an ambiguous situation: it is not clear they therefore favor paying the expenses. When such a motion arises, the chairperson or some other member should — ideally, before a second is made — point out that no motion is required in this case. Should a motion affirming the group's desire to pay the expenses subsequently arise, those opposing the action should seek to defeat it.*

6.3. Motions to "reaffirm" existing legislation, policy, or resolution should be avoided if at all possible.

6.3.1. Motions to "reaffirm" have little effect if passed, but create an ambiguous situation if they fail.

6.4. Generally, motions to "accept" or "approve" informational reports should be avoided.

6.4.1. It is usually unnecessary for the group to take any formal action to receive the information contained in the report.

6.4.2. Technically, if the group agrees, by motion or unanimous consent, to accept or approve a report, it is agreeing to the accuracy of the report's contents and conclusions or to any recommendations the report may contain.

6.4.3. If the group wishes to acknowledge formally or express appreciation for the effort behind the report, it should do so in a carefully worded resolution to that effect.

6.5. Most motions must be seconded.

> *NOTE: "Motions" that do not need a second usually take the form of requests, orders, inquiries, and points of order that enable individual members to protect their rights or to require that expected procedures be followed. Refer to the discussion of "Incidental motions" in Appendix A and to the chart in Appendix B to determine which motions do not need a second.*

6.5.1. A second is an expression by a member other than the maker of the motion that the motion is worth discussing.

6.5.2. The seconder of a motion is not necessarily in favor of the motion, nor is s/he committed to vote for it or argue for it.

6.5.3. If discussion begins even though the motion has not been seconded, the discussants have *de facto* seconded the motion and the motion is in order.

> *EXPLANATION: Even though some such expression as "I second the motion," or "second" is not used, a member, by making a comment supporting or opposing the measure, has performed the function of a second as indicated in 6.5.1. However, questions that seek clarification as to the motion's meaning or intent should not be taken as "seconds." Once a motion has been passed, it cannot be voided by noting that it was never seconded.*

6.5.4. Once discussion has begun on a motion, "withdrawing" a second is of no consequence. The motion is still in order and pending.

6.5.5. A motion submitted by a committee, a majority of whose members are also members of the parent body, is presumed to have at least two members of the parent body believing it to be worth discussing and a second from the floor is not required.

6.6. To become pending before the group — i.e., to claim the group's attention — motions must be moved, seconded, and then stated by the chairperson.

6.6.1. Prior to its being seconded, a motion that has been made is not yet pending before the group. It belongs only to the maker and s/he is free to withdraw it or change it as s/he sees fit. A motion included on the agenda that is to be made by an individual may be changed or withdrawn by the individual prior to its being submitted to the group.

6.6.2. A motion included on the agenda that is to be made by a committee may be withdrawn or changed by the committee prior to its being brought before the group by the chairperson.

6.6.3. When a motion has been made, seconded, and then stated by the chairperson (typically with such language as "It is moved and seconded that..."), it then belongs to the group and can be changed or withdrawn only with the consent of the group. At this stage of the process, the motion is said to be "pending" —i.e., legitimately claiming the attention of the group, and must be disposed of by group action.

6.6.3.1. In the event that discussion on a motion begins without the motion having been stated by the chairperson, the motion is regarded as having *de facto* become pending.

6.6.3.2. Once a motion has become pending, its maker cannot withdraw it without the permission of the group. Such permission is ordinarily granted by unanimous consent, but if the withdrawal is controversial, permission to withdraw must be put to a vote with a majority of the votes cast favoring withdrawal. (*See Appendix A for a discussion of the incidental motion, "withdraw a motion."*)

6.6.3.3. Once a motion has become pending, it can be changed only with the consent of the group. Often changes are made by unanimous consent, but if a change is controversial, it may require a formal motion to amend with a second and a majority vote needed to approve the change. One **misunderstanding** of the amending process is for a member to suggest a "friendly amendment" to the motion's maker as though it were up to the maker to approve the change once the motion is pending.

EXPLANATION: When a member other than the maker of a motion believes that an alteration would improve the motion, s/he should suggest that the group approve the change rather than ask the motion's maker for approval. While many alterations to pending motions are made informally and without controversy by unanimous consent, it is up to the group —not the maker of the motion— to approve the change.

6.7. Motions must be in order.

6.7.1. Motions that propose substantive decisions such as resolutions and ordinances are not in order if they are not clearly listed on the notice for the meeting.

6.7.2. In general, motions are not in order that propose substantially the same action as a motion decided previously in the same meeting. If it seems desirable to revisit an issue disposed of earlier in the meeting, a motion to reconsider should be used. There must be some basis, such as new information or insight, to reconsider the original matter.

6.7.3. A motion is not in order if another motion of higher rank is pending before the group.

6.7.3.1. Main motions (e.g., resolutions and ordinances) are lowest in rank and cannot be made when any other motion is pending. The motions to reconsider, rescind, and take from the table are regarded as main motions as far as the ranking of motions is concerned.

6.7.3.2. Subsidiary motions apply to the handling of main motions and are in order when a main motion is pending but not when a privileged motion is pending.

6.7.3.3. Subsidiary motions are ranked in relation to each other in accordance with the list below. A motion listed lower on the list is not in order when any one of those listed above it is pending.

Table (or "lay on the table")
Close debate (or "move the previous question")

Limit or Extend Debate
Postpone to Specific Time
Refer to Committee
Amend
Postpone Indefinitely

(See Appendix A for a full discussion of subsidiary motions.)

6.7.3.4. Privileged motions have to do with important aspects of the event of the meeting itself. Any privileged motion can be made while a main motion or a subsidiary motion is pending.

6.7.3.5. Privileged motions are ranked in relation to each other in accordance with the list below. Any motion listed lower on the list is not in order when any one of those listed above it is pending.

Set an Adjourned Meeting ("fix the time to which to adjourn")
Adjourn
Recess
Request a Privilege
Call for the Orders of the Day

(See Appendix A for a full discussion of privileged motions.)

6.7.3.6. Incidental motions are situation-specific. They have no rank among themselves but when an incidental motion is relevant to the immediate situation, it is in order when a motion of another class or even another incidental motion is pending. However, an incidental motion may not be made when the business of another incidental motion is being considered.

6.7.3.7. Many incidental motions are not motions in the customary sense but, rather, are requests, inquiries, orders, and appeals. The most common incidental motions are listed below.

- Parliamentary Inquiry
- Request Information
- Point of Order
- Division of the Assembly
- Division of the Question
- Appeal from the Decision of the Chair
- Consider by Paragraph or Seriatim
- Suspend the Rules
- Withdraw a Motion
- Object to Consideration

(See Appendix A for a fuller discussion of incidental motions.)

6.7.4. Upon disposing of a motion of higher rank that was made when a motion of lower rank is pending, the group returns its attention immediately to the lower ranking motion.

6.8. Some motions are not debatable.

6.8.1. While the rules of procedure generally tend to encourage discussion and debate, traditional manuals regard some motions as "undebatable" on the grounds that there is nothing to debate or that to debate a motion would be contrary to its intent.

> *EXPLANATION: For example, motions to close debate or limit debate seek to expedite the conduct of business. To debate them would delay the conduct of business. See Appendix B for a listing of motions that are not debatable.*

6.9. Some motions are amendable.

6.9.1. Motions that propose actions that can be quantitatively or qualitatively varied are amendable.

6.9.1.1. Motions that cannot be quantitatively or qualitatively varied are not amendable. *(See Appendix B for a listing of motions that are not amendable.)*

6.9.1.2. Once a motion is pending, only the group, not the motion's maker, may decide to amend it. Amendment is a group decision. *(See 6.6.3.3. above.)*

6.9.2. Amendments must be germane to the action proposed in the pending motion.

6.9.2.1. If the relevance of a proposed amendment to the pending motion is not clear, the group may decide whether to admit it.

6.9.2.1.1. The chairperson may rule a proposed amendment out of order on the grounds that it is not germane to the pending motion. Such ruling is subject to appeal and the appeal may result in a group decision as to whether or not to overturn the chair's ruling. *(See Appendix A for a discussion of the incidental motion, "Appeal from the decision of the chair.")*

6.9.2.1.2. If the chairperson is in doubt as to the germaneness of a proposed amendment, s/he may put the issue of germaneness to the group to decide by its vote.

6.9.2.1.3. A group's decision that an amendment is germane does not mean that the amendment has been adopted. It means only that the group regards the proposed amendment as relevant.

6.9.3. An amendment may be in order even though it is hostile to the action proposed in the motion to which applies.

6.9.3.1. An amendment is in order even if its effect would be to alter the main motion in such a way that the amended motion would propose action different from, and even at odds with, the motion to which it applies.

6.9.3.2. An amendment is out of order if its exact effect can be achieved by voting against the pending motion to which it purports to apply.

> *EXAMPLE: The motion pending before the village board directs that "the clerk be required to attend the seminar on parliamentary procedure." A motion to amend by inserting "not" before "be" ("...not be required...") would not be in order because voting "No" on the main motion would accomplish the same thing. However, it would be in order to amend the main motion by inserting "not" after "required" ("...required not to attend..."). The effect of the latter amendment — requiring that the clerk not attend — cannot be achieved by voting "No" on the main motion.*

6.9.4. A motion may be amended any number of times during the course of its deliberation.

6.9.5. Amendments themselves can be amended prior to being finally decided.

6.9.5.1. To prevent deliberations from becoming too complex, only one amendment to an amendment (secondary amendment) may be pending at one time. Once a secondary amendment has been decided, an additional secondary amendment that raises a new issue is in order.

6.9.6 Motions may be amended by inserting word(s), striking word(s), and striking and inserting word(s).

> *EXAMPLE: If the main motion is that "the clerk and the village president be reimbursed for their expenses incurred while attending the land use seminar," a member could move to amend by: (A) inserting word(s), as "mileage" before "expenses" and "only" after "expenses" — i.e., "...reimbursed for their* ***mileage*** *expenses* ***only****...;" (B) striking word(s), as in striking "and the village president," — i.e. "****the clerk be reimbursed****...;" (C) striking and inserting word(s), as in, striking the "village president" and inserting "assistant clerk" — i.e., "****the clerk and the assistant clerk be reimbursed****...."*

6.9.7. Motions may be amended by substituting an entire restatement of the motion — i.e., a substitute motion.

6.9.7.1. The substitute motion, like other forms of amendment, must be germane to the topic area but may propose a course of action quite different from the original motion.

> *EXAMPLE: During discussion on the main motion that "The clerk be required to attend a seminar on parliamentary procedure," a member believes that some education is needed by the entire board but only on a part of the general topic. S/he may move to amend the motion by substituting: "The board employ a consultant to conduct a seminar on the Open Meetings Law." The motion to substitute requires a second and, if passed, only means that the board is now considering whether to adopt the substitute motion (see 6.9.8. below).*

6.9.8. Passing a motion to amend, to amend the amendment, or to amend by substitution does not pass the main motion.

6.9.8.1. If the motion to amend or substitute passes, the amended or substitute motion is then pending. If the motion to amend or substitute fails, discussion returns to the motion that was pending when the failed motion to amend or substitute was made.

6.9.9. Previously adopted main motions — i.e., ordinances or resolutions— can be amended.

6.9.9.1. The motion to amend existing legislation, policy, or resolution is a main motion and can only be made when notice has been duly provided and when no other business is pending.

6.10. In some instances, motions once decided can be reconsidered.

6.10.1. "Reconsideration" means to reopen an issue that the group has previously decided. The earlier decision may have been either to adopt or to defeat a motion.

6.10.2. The effect of deciding to reconsider an earlier decision is to reopen the issue as though it had never been decided in the first place. When a previously decided measure is under reconsideration, it is subject to full discussion, amendment, or other action that would have been in order during its original deliberation. The issue under reconsideration will then be decided again with either the same outcome or a different outcome from the original decision.

6.10.3. Under general parliamentary law, an action can be reconsidered only in the same meeting in which it was originally decided. However, the group's own rules may provide for reconsideration either in the same or the next succeeding meeting. Reconsideration of an issue at a time later than the next regular meeting should not be permitted.

> *NOTE: The League of Wisconsin Municipalities' sample ordinances specifically provide for reconsideration at the next meeting. A group that desires such a rule but that has not adopted the League's sample ordinances should enact its own rule.*

6.10.4. If a measure is passed that enters the group into a contractual arrangement with an outside party, the group must be careful that reconsideration and possible reversal of the initial decision does not violate the rights of the contractual partner.

> *EXPLANATION: A clear case would be one in which the group decided to purchase equipment and subsequently, through its agent, entered into a purchase agreement with a provider. The group could not subsequently nullify the contractual agreement simply by reconsidering (or rescinding as in 6.11 below) its initial decision. Permission of the outside party would somehow have to be obtained.*

6.10.5. The motion to reconsider must be made by someone who voted with the prevailing side when the motion was previously decided.

6.10.5.1. If it is not possible to determine whether the maker of the motion to reconsider voted with the prevailing side, the motion should be permitted if it is otherwise in order.

6.10.5.2. The motion to reconsider may be seconded by any member, regardless of how s/he voted, or if s/he abstained, when the original motion was decided.

6.10.6. The following kinds of motions may be reconsidered:

Main motion
An affirmative vote to "postpone indefinitely"
Amend
Refer to a committee before the committee begins consideration of the referred matter
Postpone to a specific time
The unexecuted portion of a decision to limit or extend debate
Closing debate (previous question) before voting on the main question begins
Set an adjourned meeting

(See Appendix B for an indication of the motions that can be reconsidered.)

6.11. Previously adopted main motions — i.e., ordinances or resolutions — can be rescinded.

6.11.1. The motion to rescind existing legislation, policy, or resolution is a main motion and can be made only when notice has been properly issued and when no other business is pending.

6.11.2 The effect of the motion to rescind is to nullify a previously adopted policy, ordinance, or resolution.

6.11.3. The motion to rescind can be made and seconded by any member.

6.11.4. There is no time restriction on when a motion to rescind a previously adopted policy, ordinance, or resolution is in order.

6.12. Motions vary as to the votes required for passage.

6.12.1. Unless otherwise specified, a majority of the votes cast is the minimum number of votes required to pass a measure.

6.12.2. For some motions, a proportion or number of votes that would be more than a majority of the votes cast may be required by statute, the group's own rules, or the parliamentary manual.

6.12.3. For some motions, relevant statutes or the group's own rules may provide that the requirement for passage is a majority or other proportion of the members present (rather than the votes cast) or of the entire membership of the body. *(See explanation at 7.7.)*

6.13. Compound motions can be divided and their parts considered separately.

6.13.1. The group may decide — by unanimous consent or by passing the incidental motion to divide the question — to consider and decide on independent parts of a compound motion separately.

6.13.1.1. To be considered separately, the parts of the motion must be independent so that adoption or defeat of one part does not logically affect the deliberation on other part(s).

> *EXAMPLE: If the group were discussing the pending resolution to "commend the clerk for his election to the presidency of the state clerk's association and to reimburse his expenses in attending the association's meetings," the group could divide this resolution and consider the issue of commendation separately from reimbursement, perhaps eventually approving both, or neither, or one but not the other.*

6.13.2. The group may decide — by unanimous consent or by passing the incidental motion to consider by paragraph or seriatim — separate parts of complex motions, such as those in resolution form.

6.13.2.1. When considering a motion or resolution by seriatim or paragraph, the separate parts are discussed individually, and may be amended by group action, but not finally adopted. After each part has been considered separately, the whole document is open for further discussion, amendment, and adoption.

EXAMPLE: A city council may be considering an ordinance consisting of a set of rules that will govern its meetings. Each rule could be considered for possible amendment or possible deletion separately from the others. However, no rule is adopted until all have been considered, at which time any part of the document is open for deliberation and further amendment. Ultimately, the document as a whole is either adopted or rejected.

6.14. Specific rules for the handling of motions may vary from motion to motion and across situations.

NOTE: Consult the chart in Appendix B to determine which motions need to seconded, whether they are debatable, whether they can be amended, the vote required under general parliamentary law, and whether they can be reconsidered.

7. RULES OF DECISION-MAKING AND VOTING

The important decisions of a public body should be made through a counted and recorded voting process.

7.1. Local governments should avoid a process that requires that they achieve "consensus" or unanimity.

7.1.1. Consensus as an outcome and consensus as a process are not the same.

7.1.1.1. Consensus as an outcome means that the participants to a deliberation are in general agreement. This state of general agreement may be the result of any deliberative process.

7.1.1.2. Consensus as a process requires that deliberations be pursued until a decision is reached that is not unacceptable to any of the individual members.

7.1.2. An unqualified commitment to a consensus process is not appropriate for local governments.

7.1.2.1. A consensus process may be too time-consuming.

7.1.2.2. Group members may find it difficult to represent the wishes of their constituents at the same time they are committed to a consensus process of deliberation.

7.2. Some decisions may be made by unanimous consent.

7.2.1. Unanimous consent is a form of group decision making in which no vote is taken. Rather, the chairperson — at his/her own volition or upon the request or suggestion of a member — asks the group if there is any objection to a certain course of action or decision. If there is no objection, the chairperson "orders" the action to be taken or that the decision has been made. If a member(s) objects, the decision or action can still be taken or made, but only through a formal vote.

7.2.2. Unanimous consent is a valid form of decision-making unless some other form is explicitly required.

7.2.3. Unanimous consent as a decision-making process is a useful expediency for routine or apparently noncontroversial decisions.

> *EXAMPLE: One clear case in which unanimous consent is often used is in approving minutes of previous meetings. The chairperson often says something like "The minutes have been distributed. Are there corrections to be made? (In other words, does anyone object to approving them in their current form?) Since there are no corrections, the minutes are approved as distributed." Similarly, unanimous consent is often used to agree to amendments made spontaneously from the floor during debate on a pending motion. The chairperson might say something like, "Ms. Roberts suggests that the motion be changed to specify that the pickup we are considering have a V-8 engine. Is there any objection to this change in the motion? Since there is no objection, the motion will be changed to specify a V-8 engine." Of course, if anyone did object, the only way the motion could be amended would be through the formal process of a motion to amend. (NOTE: When amending by unanimous consent, care must be taken that the amending process doesn't become so casual that the exact wording or intent is lost.)*

7.2.4. Unanimous consent is not an appropriate mode of decision-making for ordinances, resolutions, and other substantive and important local government decisions that are best conducted through open, counted, and recorded voting.

7.3. Some decisions may be made by voice vote.

7.3.1. In taking a voice vote, the chairperson asks for both the affirmative ("aye") and the negative ("no") responses to the question of whether the motion shall be passed.

7.3.2. Upon hearing the responses, the chairperson rules that either the ayes or noes prevail, i.e., whether or not the motion passes.

7.3.3. If the chairperson is unsure of the outcome of the voice vote, s/he may take the vote in a visible and/or counted form.

7.3.4. Any member may order that the vote be retaken in a visible form.

> *NOTE: See Appendix A for a discussion of the incidental motion, "call for a division of the assembly" or "division," which entitles any member to require that a voice vote be taken in some visible form, usually a show of hands. Also, see 7.5. below for a discussion of the Open Meetings Law provision entitling any member to demand a recorded vote.*

7.3.5. Voice voting is not an appropriate form of decision-making for ordinances, resolutions, and other substantive and important local government decisions that are best made by visible, counted and recorded voting.

7.4. Most local government decisions should be made by a counted vote.

7.4.1. Counted votes may be taken by members raising their hands or standing, by roll call, or counted ballot, or machine.

7.4.2. When the chairperson announces the results of a counted vote, s/he should state whether the motion passes or fails and the number of votes for each side. The outcome as well as the number of votes on each side should be made part of the record of the meeting.

7.5. Some votes require that record of each member's vote be kept.

7.5.1. Wisconsin's Open Meetings Law provides that any member may require a vote to be taken in such a manner that the vote of each member is known and entered into the record of the meeting.

7.5.2. The group's own rules may require that recorded votes be taken on some issues.

7.5.3. Recorded votes must be taken on decisions to close the meeting to the public.

7.5.4. Recorded votes may be taken by machine, by calling the roll, or by signed ballots.

7.5.4.1. If recorded votes are taken by signed ballot, the ballot of each member must be disclosed at the end of the voting process and entered into the record of the meeting.

7.6. Secret ballots are not permitted in local government voting except when electing officers of the group. *(See 7.13.)*

7.7. More than a majority of the votes cast may be required to pass a measure.

7.7.1. On selected issues, the proportion of votes needed to pass the measure may be more than a majority. For example, two-thirds, three-fourths, or some other proportion may be required by a statute, the group's own rules, or its parliamentary manual.

7.7.2. On selected issues, a proportion or number of members voting that would be more than simply the number of votes cast —e.g., a majority (or larger proportion) of the members present or of the total number of members— may be required by statute or the group's own rules.

EXPLANATION: If the number of votes required to pass a particular measure is not specified, it is understood to be a majority of those voting. Given the possibility of absences and abstentions, a small minority could pass motions binding on the entire group. If the motion in question is not a main motion (i.e., does not involve a resolution or ordinance), and affects only those members assembled for this meeting (as in kinds of motions other than main motions as discussed in Appendix A), this low threshold required for passage may be appropriate. However, when exercising the governance function of passing resolutions and ordinances, such power in the hands of a small minority may be undesirable. Accordingly, statutes or group rules may require higher thresholds for passage by requiring that more than a majority favor the issue and/or that more members than simply those voting be taken into account. Thus, the votes required for passage in a given case could be a majority or some other proportion of: 1) the votes cast; 2) the members present; or 3) the total membership. Sometimes the vote requirement to pass a particular measure is expressed as a specific number (e.g., seven members of the council).

In determining the number of votes required to pass particular measures:

a. Be familiar with statutory requirements for the particular unit of government;

b. Be familiar with the group's own rules;

c. Remember that when a main motion (resolution or ordinance) is involved, a quorum must vote (see 2.5. above); and

d. Remember, an abstention is not a vote (see 7.11. below).

7.8. Negative votes must be called for.

7.8.1. No matter how one-sided the outcome may seem following the call for affirmative votes, negative votes must be called for. Members have the right to express themselves through voting whether they are on the prevailing side or not.

7.9. Members must be present to vote.

7.9.1. Members must be present at the meeting either in person or via telecommunication *(as in 2.8.)* in order to vote.

7.9.2. Members of local government units may not vote by proxy or absentee ballot.

7.10. A member may change his/her vote before the result is announced.

7.10.1. A member has the right to change his/her vote before the result is announced.

7.10.2. After the results of the vote are announced, a member must receive the permission of the group to change his/her vote.

7.11. Any member may abstain from voting at any time.

7.11.1. A member has the right to abstain from voting whenever s/he so desires.

> *EXPLANATION: A recent court decision [Wrzeski v. City of Madison, 558 F. Supp. (W.D. Wis. 1983)] held that a city council's rule requiring that all alderpersons must vote on every issue unless they were in a conflict of interest violated the alderperson's first amendment rights of free speech in that it compelled speech in the form of a vote. By extension, it would seem that a rule requiring a member to divulge his/her reasons for abstaining would also violate free speech rights.*

7.11.2. An abstention is not a vote.

7.11.2.1. When responding to a roll call vote with "here" or "present," a member only indicates his/her presence, which may be useful in establishing the presence of a quorum at the time the vote was taken. The member is not regarded as having voted.

> *NOTE: If the vote requirement for passage is a majority (or some other proportion) of the members present or of the total membership, an abstention has the effect of voting "no" in that it reduces the pool of possible "yes" votes.*

7.11.3. A member must abstain from voting on an issue in which s/he has a conflict of interest.

7.12. The outcome of a vote may not be called unanimous if any member abstains.

7.12.1. The measure may be said to pass (or fail) without negative (or affirmative) vote.

7.13. Voting to elect officers of the group requires special procedures.

7.13.1. Unlike other votes taken by public bodies, electing officers of the group can be done by secret ballot.

7.13.2. Appointing committees and filling vacancies is not the same as electing officers and cannot be done by secret ballot.

7.13.3. Provisions should be made to resolve tied votes.

7.13.1. It is recommended that the group's own rules provide that, in the event of a tie vote when electing officers, the vote(s) be retaken a limited number of times.

7.13.2. If the specified number of re-votes (e.g., three or four), does not resolve the issue, the group should provide that the election be decided by drawing lots or flipping a coin.

7.14. Provisions should be made to accommodate plurality votes.

7.14.1. If there are three or more candidates for a particular office, the group should decide whether or not it wishes to have the outcome decided by a plurality (i.e., the winner receiving the most votes but not a majority of the votes cast).

7.14.2. If the group does not want the winner to be determined by a plurality, it should retake the vote a limited number of times, after which it should settle on a procedure to reduce the number of candidates until one receives a majority or until only two remain.

APPENDIX A: Characteristics of Individual Motions

This section will describe the common motions in the Robert's system. They will be taken up one class at a time in accordance with the classifications alluded to in Section 6.7. The description will include the purpose or effect of each motion and its particular characteristics such as whether it needs a second, whether it is debatable and/or amendable, the vote required for adoption, and whether it can be reconsidered. The chart of motions in Appendix B summarizes these characteristics.

MAIN MOTIONS

A main motion "...is a motion whose introduction brings business before the assembly" [Robert, p. 97]. For a unit of local government, main motions are the means by which the group performs its primary governance function — i.e., passing, amending, or rescinding ordinances and resolutions. Some main motions are like motions of other classes. For example, a main motion to limit debate on an issue is like the subsidiary motion to "limit or extend the limits of debate." If the decision to limit or alter the rules of debate is made when no other motion is pending, it is a main motion. If it is intended to apply to a motion that is already pending, it is a subsidiary motion.

Main motions are in order only when no other motion is pending. Main motions are the lowest ranking of all classes of motions. They cannot be made when any other motion is pending, even another main motion. A main motion will yield to any subsidiary, privileged, or incidental motion that is otherwise in order.

Main motions are not in order if they introduce essentially the same subject that has been decided previously in the same meeting. A motion that involves the same general issue as a motion that has previously been voted down in the same meeting must propose a different action on the part of the group.

If new information or other circumstances make it desirable to revisit a motion previously decided in the same meeting, the proper procedure is to move to **reconsider** the matter. A motion to reconsider may be made only by a person voting on the prevailing side when the motion was originally decided. Whether or not to reconsider the previously decided motion is a group decision requiring a majority of those voting to agree to the reconsideration.

> *NOTE: The League of Wisconsin Municipalities' suggested ordinances governing rules for meetings permits reconsideration of a matter in the same meeting that it was originally decided or in the next succeeding regular meeting. The Robert's system limits reconsideration to the same meeting in which the measure was initially decided. The group should have its own rule in place as to whether it will permit reconsideration of an issue in any meeting later than the one in which it was initially decided.*

The introduction of a main motion does not necessarily constitute the group's first involvement with a particular matter. If a motion is voted down in one meeting, it can be **renewed** in a later meeting, subject to the constraints of the group's agenda-setting process. If a motion was laid on the table in one meeting, the group may agree to **take it from the table** later in the same meeting or in the next regular meeting. If a motion is passed in one meeting, it can be **rescinded** or **amended** at any future meeting. The group may not, however, use the main motions "to rescind," "to amend a previously adopted matter," or "to reconsider" to unilaterally negate contractual agreements with outside parties. *(See 6.10.4.)*

In addition, the group may not take a motion from the table, or rescind or amend a motion already passed, unless the notice for the meeting indicates that such action may occur.

Main motions:

*__Require a second__, except if it is made as a recommendation by a committee a majority of whose members are members of the parent body [see 6.4.5.]. Should discussion on a main motion begin without the motion having been seconded, the motion is regarded as having been *de facto* seconded. [See 6.4.3.]

*__Are debatable__. Note that certain actions — e.g., limiting debate — are not debatable when proposed as subsidiary motions that apply to motions already pending but are debatable when they take the form of a main motion, as in the case of setting up rules in advance for deliberation on a certain motion or on a specific issue.

*__Are amendable__ unless they simply contain no variable capable of amendment.

*Unless otherwise specified, main motions **require a majority of the votes cast for passage.** Local governments should be aware some measures may require more than a majority of those voting for passage. Statutes or the group's own rules may provide that the proportion of votes cast be more than a majority (e.g., two-thirds) and/or that the group of voters involved be the whole group or all of those present, rather than just those who are present and voting.

*__Can be reconsidered__ within the constraints noted above.

SUBSIDIARY MOTIONS

Subsidiary motions propose ways to handle other motions prior to or instead of voting on them directly.

Usually, subsidiary motions apply to and take precedence over pending main motions. However, the subsidiary motions to amend, to limit or extend limits of debate, and to close debate can be applied to other, higher ranking motions and to other subsidiary motions as well. Further, the motion to reconsider can be applied to some previously decided subsidiary motions.

Subsidiary motions have a ranking among themselves; that is, some subsidiary motions will take precedence over other pending subsidiary motions.

Subsidiary motions are described below in order from the lowest ranking to the highest ranking. That is, the motions described in the earlier paragraphs below will yield to those described in later paragraphs.

Postpone Indefinitely

A motion to postpone indefinitely proposes that the group stop its deliberations on a pending main motion with no expectation that the group will ever take up the matter again. If the motion to postpone indefinitely passes, the motion to which it applies is simply dropped from deliberation as though it had been voted down. If the issue is to come up again, the motion to postpone indefinitely will have to be reconsidered or the main motion will have to be reintroduced in a later meeting subject to the constraints of the group's agenda-setting process.

Postpone indefinitely:

*__Requires a second__. Should discussion begin without a second, the motion should be regarded as *de facto* seconded.

*__Is open to discussion and debate__ which can include the merits of the main motion to which it applies.

*__Is not amendable.__

*Unless otherwise specified, **requires a majority of the votes cast for passage.**

*__An affirmative vote on the motion to postpone indefinitely can be reconsidered__ later in the same meeting. A negative vote cannot be reconsidered.

Amend

A motion to amend proposes to change the wording and/or the action proposed by a pending motion. If the motion to amend is adopted, the pending motion is altered accordingly and is then subject to further deliberation and/or amendment. Note that adopting the motion to amend does not adopt the motion to which applies. *(See 6.9.)*

The motion to amend:

*__Requires a second__. Should discussion begin without a second, the motion should be regarded as *de facto* seconded.

*__Is open to discussion and debate__ if the motion to which it applies is debatable.

*__Can be amended__ with limitations as to procedure. *(See 6.9.)*
*Unless otherwise specified, **requires a majority of the votes cast for adoption,** even if the motion to which it applies requires a larger proportion or a larger pool of members.
*__Can be reconsidered__ later in the same meeting.

Refer to a Committee

The motion to refer a matter to a committee proposes that the pending motion be delegated to a committee for consideration. Specific instructions to the committee, such as when to report and what specifically to consider should be in the motion to refer. In addition, if the motion proposes to refer the matter to a group to be selected (i.e., to a "special committee") rather than to an existing committee, the motion to refer should either contain the names of the persons to comprise the committee or specify how they are to be selected — e.g., to be appointed by the chair. If the motion to refer passes, the issue in its present state is sent to the committee and the parent body stops deliberating on the issue until the committee reports. Any pending amendments to the motion will also go to the committee for consideration. Matters referred to a committee are made "orders of the day" for the meeting in which the report is due. If the motion to refer does not specify when the committee is to report, the committee should plan to report at the next regular meeting. If the parent body desires to bring the matter back to itself prior to the time of the committee report, or if the parent body is dissatisfied with the committee's progress, it may move to "discharge the committee," the effect of which is to bring the matter back to the parent body immediately. However, if the referred matter is brought back to the parent body by "discharging the committee," the parent body cannot deliberate the matter at that time unless it is on the agenda. If it is not on the agenda, the parent body will have to delay consideration until a later meeting so that proper notice can be issued.

The motion to refer a matter to a committee:
*__Requires a second__. Should discussion begin without a second, the motion should be regarded as *de facto* seconded.
*__Is debatable__.
*__Is amendable.__
*Unless otherwise specified, **requires a majority of the votes cast for adoption.**
*__Can be reconsidered__ but only before the committee actually takes up the referred

matter. Thereafter, the parent body must discharge the committee if it desires to deliberate the matter itself prior to the committee's report.

Postpone to Specified Time

Unlike the motion to postpone a matter indefinitely, the motion to postpone a matter to a specified time is used when the group wants to set the issue aside temporarily but definitely wants it to come back to their attention in the future. The motion should specify the future time — either in the same meeting or in a later meeting — that the group intends to take up the matter again. If the group passes the motion to postpone to a specified time, the matter is set aside in its present form but is ordered to return to the group's attention at the specified time. Failure to take up the issue at the time to which it was postponed would be a violation that could be corrected by the privileged motion, "call for the orders of the day" *(See below)*. The group must return to the postponed issue at the prescribed time. It may, however, postpone the issue again.

If the matter is to return to the group later in the same meeting, the hour or place on the agenda should be specified in the motion to postpone. If the matter is to return to the group in a later meeting, the date of the meeting should be specified. The group may also specify the particular time of day or placement on the agenda of the postponed issue. The motion to postpone to a specified time should not merely indicate a later event after which the postponed matter will be taken up (e.g., postpone the bond issue until after the elections). To do so would insufficiently prescribe exactly when the matter is supposed to be brought back.

The motion to postpone to a specified time:
*__Requires a second__. Should discussion begin without a second, the motion should be regarded as *de facto* seconded.
*__Is open to discussion and debate__.
*__Can be amended__ by altering the time at which the postponed matter is to be brought back.
*Unless otherwise specified, **requires a majority of the votes cast for adoption.**
*__Can be reconsidered__ in the same meeting in which it was initially decided.

Limit or Extend Limits of Debate

A unit of local government may or may not have in place rules of its own governing the number of times a member may speak on a particular issue or the length of each speech.

If the group does have such rules, this motion is used to change them by extending or limiting the number of speeches or their length.

If the group does not have such rules, this motion could be used to impose them for the deliberations on a particular issue or for a particular meeting.

This motion is a subsidiary motion if it is made while another motion(s) is pending. If it is made while a series of motions is pending — as in the case of pending main motion and a pending amendment — the motion to limit or extend limits of debate will apply only to the immediately pending motion unless it clearly specifies that all pending motions are to be affected.

If the motion to limit or extend limits of debate is made when no motion is pending but is intended to apply to issue(s) to be taken up later in the meeting, it is a main motion. Again, the motion should clearly specify the motion(s) to which it is intended to apply.

The motion to limit or extend limits of debate:
***Requires a second.**
***Is not open to discussion and debate.**
***Can be amended** by proposing extension or limitations of different time intervals.
*Unless otherwise specified, **2/3 of the votes cast is required for adoption.**
***Can be reconsidered**.

Close Debate (Move the Previous Question)

The motion to close debate (or move the previous question) is a group decision to end discussion on the pending issue(s) and to vote on them immediately. If the motion is made when a series of motions is pending — as in the case of a main motion and an immediately pending amendment — the motion to close debate will apply only to debate on the amendment unless the motion specifically includes all pending motions.

The effect of the motion to close debate is to preclude any further discussion and debate on the motion(s) to which it applies and to order that those matters be put to an immediate vote.

> *NOTE: the decision to close debate is a group decision and one member cannot by "calling the question" order that discussion stop. One member's "call for the question" may be regarded as a motion but it would still need to be approved by the group either by unanimous consent or by a two-thirds vote. (See 5.8.)*

The motion to close debate:
***Requires a second.**
***Is not open to discussion and debate.**
***Is not amendable.**
*Unless otherwise specified, **two-thirds of the votes cast is required for passage.**
***Can be reconsidered only before any vote is taken on the motion(s) to which it applies.** After any vote is taken on any one of a series of pending motions, the motion to close debate cannot be reconsidered.

Table (Lay on the Table)

The motion to table is a group decision to set aside a pending main motion and any adhering subsidiary motions without specifying whether or when the motion shall be taken up again.

Note the differences among the motion to table, the motion to postpone indefinitely and the motion to postpone to a specified time. The motion to table was originally intended to enable the group to set aside a pending matter in order to respond to an unexpected but very important issue. To use this motion for other purposes — perhaps instead of the motion to postpone indefinitely as a way to "kill" a proposal — is inappropriate. Unlike the motion to postpone indefinitely, the motion to table is not debatable. Thus, if the motion to table is used to "kill" a main motion, the group would be prevented from discussing the main motion.

The motion to table cannot apply to pending subsidiary motions without applying to the main motion to which they adhere.

If a motion is tabled, further group action is required to take it from the table. The motion to take a tabled matter from the table may be made later in the same meeting during which it was tabled or in the next regular meeting. After the next regular meeting, the tabled motion must be renewed according to group's agenda-setting process.

Units of local governments should be cautious not to remove and deliberate a tabled matter in the regular meeting following the one in which it was tabled unless the issue is included in the meeting's notice.

The motion to table:
***Requires a second.**
***Is not open to discussion and debate.**
*Is not amendable.
*Unless otherwise specified, **a majority of the votes cast is required for adoption.**
***Cannot be reconsidered**.

PRIVILEGED MOTIONS

Privileged motions do not apply to other motions that are immediately pending. Rather, they raise matters of such potentially high importance that they are entitled to take precedence over pending main and subsidiary motions.

It should be noted, however, that the subsidiary motion to amend can be applied to some pending privileged motions provided they contain a variable which is subject to amendment.

Privileged motions have a ranking among themselves, i.e., some privileged motions will take precedence over others. The privileged motions listed below are listed in reverse order of precedence. Those described first will yield to those described later.

Call for the Orders of the Day

A "call for the orders of the day" is used by a member to point out that s/he believes the agenda is not being followed or that a general or special order for the current meeting is being neglected. *(See 4.7.5)*

Upon hearing the call for the orders of the day, the chairperson, if s/he agrees the call is accurate, must take action to bring the proper matter before the group. If the chairperson believes the member calling for the orders of the day is incorrect, s/he will rule accordingly, subject to appeal. If the chairperson believes there is good reason to depart from the orders of the day, s/he may put the matter to a vote of the group. Two-thirds of those voting must agree to depart from the orders of the day.

A call for the orders of the day:
*__Need not be seconded.__
*__Is not open to discussion and debate.__
*__Cannot be amended.__
*__No vote is taken unless__ the group decides to depart from the orders of the day, in which case **two-thirds of those voting must agree.**
*__Cannot be reconsidered__.

Raise a Question of Privilege

Raising a question of privilege is a device that enables a member to interrupt pending business (other than business specifically relating to one of the three privileged motions ranking above it) with a request or a motion that s/he believes to be urgent to justify immediate attention. For example, a member may raise a question of privilege to request or move that the behavior of onlookers be controlled or that some aspect of discomfort, such as room temperature, be attended to.

If the chairperson believes the request is simple and noncontroversial, s/he may order it fulfilled, subject to the appeal of other member(s) who may be in disagreement. If the chairperson believes the request is not sufficiently urgent to interrupt pending business, s/he may deny it or delay it, subject to appeal. The chairperson may also ask that the request be put in the form of a motion, thus leaving it to the group to decide whether to grant the request. *(See 4.5.)*

> *NOTE: If the request is put in motion form, it would be a main motion with all the characteristics of such.*

Raising a question of privilege:
*__Need not be seconded.__
*__Is not open to discussion and debate.__
*__Is not amendable.__
*__Is ruled on by the chair,__ subject to appeal, unless the request is put in motion form.
*The chairperson's decision **cannot be reconsidered.**

Recess

A recess is a group decision to take an intermission in the meeting for a specified period of time.

A recess differs from an adjournment in that a group deciding to recess intends to reconvene at a later point within the time span the meeting might normally occupy. An adjournment ceases the present meeting, and public bodies may not meet again until public notice has been provided.

The motion or decision to recess should stipulate when the meeting will reconvene. When reconvened, the group resumes its business at the point at which it recessed.

If a recess is provided for in the printed agenda, the chair simply announces that the time for recess has arrived and declares when the meeting will reconvene. If the group does not want to recess at this predetermined time, it may, by two-thirds vote, decide to recess at a later time or not at all.

The motion to recess cannot be made when a motion to adjourn or a motion to set the time to which to adjourn is pending. It can, however, be made when any other motion is pending.

The motion to recess can also be made when no other motion is pending, in which case it is a main motion —not a privileged one— and has the characteristics of that class.

The privileged motion to recess:
*__Requires a second.__
*__Is not open to discussion and debate.__

*__Can be amended__ as to when the group will reconvene.
*Unless otherwise specified, **requires a majority of the votes cast for adoption.**
Cannot be reconsidered.

Adjourn

The privileged motion to adjourn is a group decision to close the meeting immediately, even though business may be pending. It is in order as a privileged motion only when a provision for the next meeting has been made, when no time for adjourning the present meeting has been determined, and if the motion itself does not specify the time at which or to which the meeting will be adjourned.

The motion to adjourn is a main motion if made: (1) when no provision is made for the next meeting; (2) when the time for adjourning the present meeting has already been determined; or (3) when the motion includes the time at which or to which the meeting will be adjourned. When it is made under any of these three conditions, the motion to adjourn has the characteristics of the class of main motions and is out of order when other business is pending.

> *NOTE: The main motion to adjourn to a specific time should not be confused with the privileged motion discussed below that sets the time to which to adjourn. The motion to adjourn to a specified time intends to adjourn the present meeting immediately. The privileged motion to set the time to which to adjourn only provides, in effect, that when the group adjourns the present meeting, it will meet again at the time proposed. Adopting this latter motion does not adjourn the present meeting.*

A motion to adjourn may not be made while a vote is being taken.

Business that is pending when meeting adjourns is taken up under "unfinished business" at the next regular or adjourned meeting.

If the time for adjournment of the present meeting is set on the agenda, the chairperson announces that the time for adjournment has arrived and, if the group is ready to adjourn, no motion to adjourn is required. The group may, however, by 2/3 of the votes cast, decide not to adjourn at the prescribed time.

The privileged motion to adjourn:
***Requires a second.**
* **Is not open to discussion and debate.** However, while a motion to adjourn is pending, it is in order to point out business that should be taken care of before adjournment, to make important announcements, to move to reconsider an item of business at the next meeting, and to move to set a time to meet before the next scheduled meeting.
***Is not amendable.**
*Unless otherwise specified, **requires a majority of the votes cast for passage.**
***Cannot be reconsidered** but may be made again after the next agenda item has been taken up.

Set the Time to Which to Adjourn

The motion to set the time to which to adjourn provides for a meeting prior to the next regularly scheduled meeting. The customary purpose is to continue business the group, for whatever reason, does not wish to do in the present meeting, but does want to attend to before the next regular meeting.

Passing the motion to set the time to which to adjourn does not adjourn the present meeting, but says in effect, "When we adjourn we will adjourn to a specified time."

The meeting created by this motion is called an adjourned meeting.

If this motion is made when no business is pending, it is a main motion and has the characteristics as such. Also, the motion to set the time of the next meeting as a main motion can be made and passed during a meeting at which no quorum is present.

As a privileged motion, the motion to set the time to which to adjourn takes precedence over any other business. Note that this motion takes precedence over the motion to adjourn so that adjournment will not prevent the group's attention to matters that should not wait for the next regular meeting.

The motion to set the time to which to adjourn:
***Requires a second.**
***Is not open to discussion and debate.**
***Can be amended** as to the time or place of the adjourned meeting.
*Unless otherwise specified, **requires a majority of the votes cast for adoption.**
* **Can be reconsidered.**

INCIDENTAL MOTIONS

Incidental motions respond to specific situations. Generally speaking, if they are relevant to the situation, they are in order and take precedence over any matter that may be pending.

There is no rank within the class of incidental motions. An incidental motion, if situationally relevant, is in order when another motion, including another incidental motion, is pending.

The first five incidental motions to be discussed below differ from other motions in that they are not, in and of themselves, proposals that the group make a particular decision or take a particular action. Rather, they are mechanisms that members can use to protect their rights of participation. The process they initiate may, however, lead to a group decision.

Parliamentary Inquiry

A parliamentary inquiry is used to exercise a member's right to be informed of the proper procedures for initiating action or otherwise responding to the deliberation of the issue at hand.

Since a parliamentary inquiry exercises a member's basic right of participation, it does not require a second and may interrupt the proceedings.

The chair is required to respond to the inquiry to the best of his/her ability and may consult with appropriate counsel or with the group before responding.

The response of the chair to an inquiry is not subject to appeal. However, a member believing the chairperson to be in error may act contrary to the chairperson's response and, if ruled out of order, may then appeal the chair's ruling.

A parliamentary inquiry:
***Does not require a second.**
***Is not open to discussion and debate** except for the limited consultation noted above.
***Is not amendable.**
***Is not decided by vote;** rather, the chair responds with an opinion.
***Cannot be reconsidered.**

Request for Information

A request for information is like a parliamentary inquiry. It is used to exercise a member's right to be as fully informed as possible on the substance of the issue at hand rather than the procedure for handling it.

Again, the chairperson is required to respond to the best of his/her ability and, to do so, may consult with others who may have the requested information.

The chairperson's response is not subject to appeal.

A request for information:
***Does not require a second.**
***Is not open to discussion and debate** except to clarify the request and to consult briefly with others as needed.
***Is not amendable.**
***Is not decided by vote;** rather, the chairperson responds with an opinion.
***Cannot be reconsidered.**

Point of Order

When a member believes that something procedurally incorrect is transpiring, s/he is said to "rise" to a point of order. Under this procedure, a member is entitled, without a second, to point out the perceived procedural impropriety and the chair is required to respond with a ruling that the member is either correct or incorrect.

If the chair rules that the member is correct, the chairperson orders the correct procedures to be followed.

If the chair rules that the member is incorrect, any member may appeal from the chair's decision *(see below)*. Under the appeal process, the decision as to what constitutes proper procedure is decided by the group and a majority of those voting can overturn the chair's ruling. A tie vote sustains the chairperson's ruling.

A point of order:

*__Does not require a second.__

*__Is not open to discussion and debate__ other than to explain the manner in which procedures are perceived to be incorrect.

*__Is not amendable.__

*Usually **is not decided by vote;** rather, the chair rules in response to the point. The chair may, however, simply put the issue of the correctness of the procedure to a vote of the group, in which case the decision is made by a majority of the votes cast. Alternatively, the chair may rule and his/her ruling may be appealed, in which case a majority of votes cast are required to overrule.

*__Cannot be reconsidered.__

Division of the Assembly

The call for a division of the assembly applies only when a voice vote has been taken. A member, upon hearing the chairperson's announcement of the outcome, may require that the vote be taken again in some visible form — usually a show of hands.

The call for a division does not require that the votes thus retaken be counted.

The call for a division of the assembly should not be confused with the right of any member of a unit of local government in Wisconsin to require that a vote be taken in such manner that the votes of each member be known and made part of the record. This latter procedure is an option contained in the Open Meetings Law and is to be ordered prior to the vote. A "division" is relevant only after a voice vote has been taken, and does not require that each member's vote be made part of the record.

A call for a division of the assembly:
***Does not require a second.**
***Is not open to discussion and debate.**
***Is not amendable.**
***No vote is taken and no ruling is made;** the chair is required to retake a vote in some visible manner.
***Cannot be reconsidered.**

Division of the Question (Separation)

A motion or resolution may propose two or more actions. If the proposals could be adopted independently of each other, they may be separated and acted on individually. *(See 6.13.)*

Robert distinguishes between questions that *may* be divided by group action and those that *must* be divided upon the demand of a single member. In the Robert system, if a motion contains separate actions related to the *same* subject, the motion *may* be divided by group action --i.e., a motion to divide that is seconded and passed by unanimous consent or majority vote. However, Robert says that a motion or resolution containing recommendations or actions relating to *different* subjects *must* be divided upon the demand of a single member.

The approach taken here is that a motion or resolution is to be divided (or separated) at the request of a single member whether the several parts relate to the same subject or not. This approach seems to be consistent with practice in units of local government. To avoid confusion, units of local desiring to separate questions upon the request of a single member should make this practice explicitly permissible in their own rules.

Note that a motion or resolution can be divided by separating as many of the different parts as desired. Each part so separated is deliberated and voted on individually, and the adoption or defeat of any of the part(s) has no bearing on the outcome of deliberations on the other parts. This differs from considering lengthy documents by paragraph or seriatim as described in a later section.

A division of the question:
***Does not require a second.**
***Is not open to discussion and debate.**
***There is nothing to amend.**
***No vote is taken;** the chair orders the separation at the request of any member.
***Cannot be reconsidered.**

Appeal from the Decision of the Chair

When a member believes the chair has made an incorrect ruling, the member may "appeal from the decision of the chair." If the appeal is seconded, the matter is put to a vote of the group with a majority of the votes cast required to overturn the chair's decision.

An appeal from the decision of the chair:
***Requires a second.**
***Is open to discussion and debate** unless it concerns a ruling having to do with the order of business or the rules of debate, or unless the immediately pending question is undebatable.
***Is not amendable.**
***Requires a majority** of the votes cast to overrule the decision of the chair.
***Can be reconsidered.**

Consider by Paragraph (Seriatim)

When a single motion or resolution contains one or more parts that are not totally independent of each other and which *in toto* comprise a single document, it is often convenient to focus on the parts, clauses, sections, or paragraphs one at a time. To do this, the group agrees to take up each part separately for purposes of debate and amendment.

Although the parts are debated and amended separately, no final decision to adopt or reject any one part is made until all have been separately debated and/or amended. Similarly, the subsidiary motions to postpone indefinitely, refer to a committee, postpone to a specific time, or table cannot be applied to any one part separately. If any of these actions are desirable, they must be applied to the entire motion or resolution.

After the group has considered each of the separate parts, the entire document becomes pending. The document as a whole, or any one part, is open to debate and further amendment. At the conclusion of the deliberations, a single vote is take on the entire document.

The motion to consider by paragraph or seriatim:
*__Requires a second.__
*__Is not debatable.__
*__Can be amended__ as to the specification of the parts to be considered separately.
*__Unless otherwise specified,__ requires approval of a majority of those voting for passage.
*__Cannot be reconsidered.__

Suspend the Rules

A group may find that one of its rules or a rule in its manual of procedure prevents it from doing what it wants to do at the time. If the rule is not necessary to protect the interests of absent members or the public and is not a statutory provision, it may be suspended with the consent of two-thirds of those voting.

Action taken to alter the order of items on the published agenda is a variation of suspending the rules. *(The listing of items on the agenda is taken as a "rule" of order.)*

As another example, the group may have no rule of its own regarding time limits on reconsideration of a matter already settled, but cites Robert's as its parliamentary authority. The group may find it desirable to reconsider the matter at the regular meeting following the one in which the matter was initially disposed of. Assuming that reconsideration of the issue would not adversely affect an outside party and that the possibility of reconsideration of the specific issue is on the agenda of the present meeting, the group could pass a motion to suspend Robert's prohibition against reconsideration in a later meeting, thus enabling the motion to reconsider to be made. Realize, of course, that in the present example, the group would have to adopt the motion to suspend rules, and then the motion to reconsider, before the issue could be taken up.

The motion to suspend the rules:
***Requires a second.**
***Is not open to discussion and debate.**
***Is not amendable.**
*Unless otherwise specified, **requires approval of two-thirds of those voting for passage.**
***Cannot be reconsidered.**

Withdraw a Motion

Contrary to popular belief and practice, withdrawing a motion is not something the maker of a motion can do unilaterally after the motion has been stated by the chair and thus becomes the property of the group. Rather, the maker of the motion must request consent of the group to withdraw the motion.

Usually, such permission is granted by unanimous consent. However, if the withdrawal is controversial, formal group action — i.e., a vote — may be necessary.

The request to withdraw a motion:
***Does not require a second to seek unanimous consent;** does require a second if unanimous consent has not been obtained and a vote to grant permission will be necessary.
***Is not subject to discussion and debate.**
***Is not amendable.**
*Unless otherwise specified, **requires a majority of the votes cast for approval.**
***A negative vote can be reconsidered.**

Object to Consideration

A member of a group may believe that a particular matter that is about to be introduced is not an appropriate issue for the group's deliberation. The perceived impropriety would usually be that the issue is outside the group's sphere of influence or jurisdiction.

Once the deliberation of an issue has begun, it is too late to object to its consideration.

Raising the objection can be done by a single member without a second; however, to sustain the objection — i.e., to agree not to consider the matter — requires a two-thirds vote.

Object to consideration:

*__Does not require a second.__

*__Is not open to discussion and debate__ other than to explain the reasons for the objection.

*__Is not amendable.__

*Unless otherwise specified **requires two-thirds of those voting for passage.**

*__The vote sustaining the objection can be reconsidered; the vote denying the objection cannot be reconsidered.__

APPENDIX B: Chart of Motions

Main Motions	Second Required	Debatable	Amendable	Vote Required	Reconsider
Ordinances & Resolutions	Yes	Yes	Yes	At Least Majority	Yes
Take from the Table	Yes	No	No	Majority	No
Reconsider	Yes	Yes	No	Majority	No
Rescind	Yes	Yes	Yes	Majority	Negative Vote Only

Subsidiary Motions	Second Required	Debatable	Amendable	Vote Required	Reconsider
Table	Yes	No	No	Majority	No
Close Debate	Yes	No	No	2/3rds	No
Limit or Extend Debate	Yes	No	Yes	2/3rds	Yes
Postpone to Specific Time	Yes	Yes	Yes	Majority	Yes
Refer to Committee	Yes	Yes	Yes	Majority	Yes
Amend	Yes	Yes	Yes	Majority	Yes
Postpone Indefinitely	Yes	Yes	No	Majority	Affirmative Vote Only

Privileged Motions	Second Required	Debatable	Amendable	Vote Required	Reconsider
Set Time to which to Adjourn	Yes	No	Yes	Majority	Yes
Adjourn	Yes	No	No	Majority	No
Recess	Yes	No	Yes	Majority	No
Raise Questions of Privilege	No	No	No	Chair Rules	No
Call for Orders of the Day	No	No	No	Chair Rules	No

Incidental Motions	Second Required	Debatable	Amendable	Vote Required	Reconsider
Parliamentary Inquiry	No	No	No	Chair Responds	No
Request Information	No	No	No	Chair Responds	No
Point of Order	No	No	No	Chair Rules	No
Division of Assembly	No	No	No	Chair Responds	No
Division of Question	No	No	No	Chair Responds	No
Appeal from Chair's Decision	Yes	Yes	No	Majority	Yes
Consider by Paragraph or Seriatim	Yes	No	Yes	Majority	No
Suspend the Rules	Yes	No	No	2/3rds	No
Withdraw a Motion	No	No	No	Majority	Negative Vote Only
Object to Consideration	No	No	No	2/3rds	Only Vote Substaining Objection

REFERENCES

Manuals

Robert, Henry M. *Robert's Rules of Order Newly Revised.* Reading, Massachusetts: Addison Wesley Longman, Inc., 1997.

Sturgis, Alice. *Sturgis's Standard Code of Parliamentary Procedure*. Second Edition. New York: McGraw-Hill Book Company, 1966.

Mason, Paul. *Mason's Manual of Legislative Procedure*. St. Paul: West Publishing Company, 1989.

Other

League of Wisconsin Municipalities. *The Conduct of Common Council Meetings: Suggested Rules of Procedure with Model Ordinance and Annotations*. Madison, Wisconsin, 1987.

League of Wisconsin Municipalities. *The Conduct of Village Board Meetings: Suggested Rules of Procedure with Model Ordinance and Annotations*. Madison, Wisconsin, 1987.

League of Wisconsin Municipalities. *The Powers and Duties of Wisconsin Mayors*. Madison, Wisconsin, 1987.

[NOTE: Contact the League of Wisconsin Municipalities at 202 State St., Suite 300, Madison, Wisconsin, 53703-2215 (608-267-2380).]

Natkins, Burt P. and James H. Schneider. *Understanding Wisconsin's Open Meetings Law*. Oregon, Wisconsin: Logos Publications, 1994. Logos Publications, 185 W. Netherwood St., Oregon, Wisconsin, 53575-1153.